THE MAILBOX® The Education Center®

Grades 4–6

Daily Journal Prompts

D1192045

Two journal prompts for every day of the year!

- **730 Holiday, Seasonal, and General Prompts for August–July**

- **Reproducible Journal Covers**

- **Reproducible Student Writing Sheet**

Managing Editor: Debra Liverman

Editorial Team: Becky S. Andrews, Kimberley Bruck, Karen P. Shelton, Diane Badden, Thad H. McLaurin, Debra Liverman, Lauren E. Cox, Peggy W. Hambright, Amy Payne, Karen A. Brudnak, Sarah Hamblet, Hope Rodgers, Dorothy C. McKinney, Rusty Fischer, Shawna Graham, Elizabeth H. Lindsay, Kim Minafo, Angela Rood, Suzette Westhoff

Production Team: Lisa K. Pitts, Donna K. Teal (COVER ARTIST), Pam Crane, Rebecca Saunders, Jennifer Tipton Cappoen, Chris Curry, Sarah Foreman, Theresa Lewis Goode, Ivy L. Koonce, Clint Moore, Greg D. Rieves, Barry Slate, Donna K. Teal, Tazmen Carlisle, Amy Kirtley-Hill, Kristy Parton, Debbie Shoffner, Cathy Edwards Simrell, Lynette Dickerson, Mark Rainey, Clevell Harris

www.themailbox.com

Table of Contents

©2005 The Mailbox® Books
All rights reserved.
ISBN10 #1-56234-626-1 • ISBN13 #978-1-56234-626-3

How to Use This Book

Make Monthly Journal Response Booklets

At the beginning of each month, make one copy of the appropriate monthly cover (see pages 100–111) for each student. Then make several copies of the lined writing page (see page 112) for each student. Stack the lined sheets of paper, place the monthly cover on top, and then staple along the left-hand side to create a booklet. Have each student decorate the cover with markers or crayons.

Use for Guided Daily Journal Writing

At the start of each day, select one of the two prompts to write on the board, or write both prompts on the board and instruct each student to select the one that interests her the most. (If you have access to an overhead projector, a transparency of the prompts will be a timesaver and can be reused year after year.) Have students write their journal entries in their monthly journal response booklets. If desired, discuss the daily writing topic with students before they begin writing.

Use for Independent Journal Writing

Post copies of a month's worth of journal prompts in a center or on a classroom bulletin board. Every day, challenge each child to select one prompt from the appropriate day to respond to in her monthly journal response booklet.

August 1

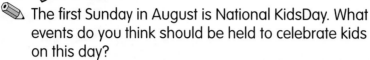

✏️ The first Sunday in August is National KidsDay. What events do you think should be held to celebrate kids on this day?

✏️ Frances Scott Key, the author of "The Star-Spangled Banner," was born on August 1, 1779. Do you think that all Americans should know the words to this song? Explain.

August 2

✏️ August is Children's Eye Health and Safety Month. Pretend that you are at the eye doctor when you find a pair of magical glasses. Write about what you see through these glasses.

✏️ The neighbor's dog has just delivered a litter of five puppies. Write a letter persuading your parent to let you have one of the puppies as a pet.

August 3

✏️ Christopher Columbus set sail for the New World on this day in 1492. Imagine being on a ship with him as he crossed the ocean. Describe what you think daily life was like.

✏️ Imagine that you are on a ship and you have discovered a new land. What would you like to name this new land? Write a letter convincing your captain to use the name you suggest.

Dear Captain,

August 4

✏️ Do you think that your school cafeteria should sell soft drinks? Explain.

✏️ Describe the ultimate tree house. What would it look like, and what would you have in it?

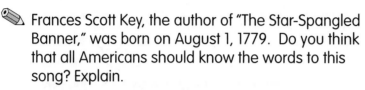
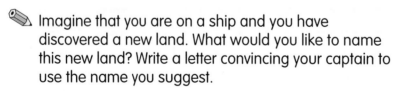
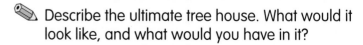

August 5

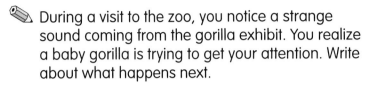

✏️ August is National Inventors' Month. Imagine that you could personally thank one inventor for his or her invention. Who would you thank? Explain.

✏️ During a visit to the zoo, you notice a strange sound coming from the gorilla exhibit. You realize a baby gorilla is trying to get your attention. Write about what happens next.

August 6

✏️ Your family is driving to your favorite summer vacation spot when you come upon a roadblock and detour sign. You decide to take the detour. Write about what happens next. Where do you end up?

✏️ Some schools have several short vacation breaks during the year instead of one long summer break. List the pros and cons of each. Which do you prefer? Explain.

August 7

✏️ The first Saturday in August is National Mustard Day. Explain how to build the most delicious submarine sandwich. Don't forget the mustard!

✏️ A flower? A seed? A fruit? Where do you think mustard comes from? Explain how you think mustard is made.

August 8

✏️ Think of an event in your life that didn't work out the way you thought it would. Rewrite the event and give it a new ending.

✏️ Imagine that you are a red-carpet reporter at the Academy Awards. If you could interview one movie star, who would you choose? Explain.

August 9

✏️ After a long day of swimming, you're hungry for a sweet snack. Describe how to make your favorite refreshing afternoon dessert.

✏️ Imagine that all the instruments in the band could talk. What do you think they would say to each other? Write a conversation two of the instruments might have with each other.

August 10

✏️ Herbert Hoover, the 31st president of the United States, was born on this day in 1874. If you could have given some advice to a past president, what advice would that be?

✏️ The astronauts have decided to take a civilian with them on their next trip to the moon. What should be the criteria for choosing the lucky person?

August 11

✏️ Create a slogan that you would use to describe summer. Explain your choice of words.

✏️ Imagine that as you're riding your bike down the street, it suddenly grows wings and lifts you off the ground. Where does it take you? What do you do?

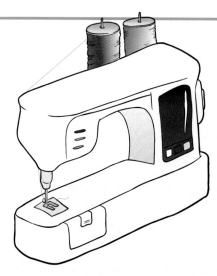

August 12

✏️ The home sewing machine was invented on this day in 1851. If you were a skilled tailor and could sew anything, what would you make? Explain.

✏️ Due to the hot summer temperatures, there is a citywide power outage. You and your friends are sitting in your dark and quiet living room. How will you pass the time and stay cool?

August 13

 In some countries children your age have to work to help their families. Should young children be allowed to work? Explain.

 What one electronic device could you not live without? Explain.

August 14

 National Garage Sale Day is the second Saturday in August. Write a story about a wacky garage sale adventure.

 Imagine that while on a camping trip with friends, you are sitting around a campfire telling scary stories. Suddenly you hear the bushes move. Write about what happens next.

August 15

 Today is National Relaxation Day. Describe your idea of a relaxing day.

 The first transcontinental railroad was completed on this day in 1870. It connected the Atlantic and Pacific oceans. Before the railroad was created, people traveled for months in covered wagons to cross this area. Imagine that you are riding in a wagon train traveling west. Describe a day on your journey.

August 16

 The third week in August is Reduce the Clutter Week. Imagine that your parents have told you to clean out your room. Besides your furniture, you may only keep five items. List the items you will keep and explain why you can't bear to part with them.

 You are getting a group together to look for buried treasure. Create a help wanted ad to find workers. Be sure to include the time, date, place, and any equipment needed.

August 17

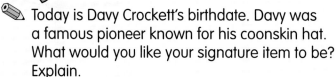

✏️ Today is Davy Crockett's birthdate. Davy was a famous pioneer known for his coonskin hat. What would you like your signature item to be? Explain.

✏️ Pretend that you are at the beach making a sand castle. As you are digging the moat for your castle, you find something that looks like part of a pirate's treasure. Write about what happens next.

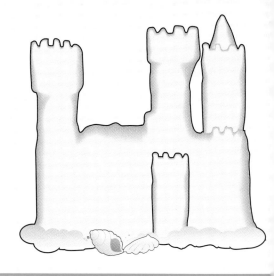

August 18

✏️ Describe what you think a kitchen is like in a submarine.

✏️ What is your favorite type of dessert? Write a descriptive paragraph about a world made of this sweet treat.

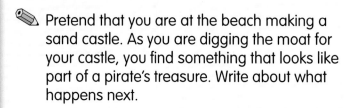

August 19

✏️ National Aviation Day is August 19. List as many forms of transportation as you can. Explain which form you prefer to use when traveling.

✏️ Imagine that you and your family are visiting a museum and are accidentally locked inside. Write about what happens next.

August 20

✏️ Imagine that you are a watermelon in a watermelon patch. How would you persuade a child to take you home?

✏️ "You can't teach an old dog new tricks" is a common saying. Do you think someone can ever become too old to learn new things? Explain.

August 21

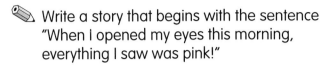

✎ Make a list of your favorite things about summer. Write a poem using at least five of the things you listed.

✎ Write a story that begins with the sentence "When I opened my eyes this morning, everything I saw was pink!"

August 22

✎ In honor of National Punctuation Day, write a letter to a friend using no punctuation or capitalization. In the letter, explain why capitalization and punctuation are important.

✎ In your opinion, which punctuation mark is the most important? Why?

August 23

✎ Pretend you have been invited to travel with the circus for a week. What kind of performer would you choose to be? What happens on your first night in front of the crowd?

✎ What do you like most about your personality? Explain.

August 24

✎ What is one thing that you would like to teach someone else? Explain.

✎ Imagine that you could communicate with any one animal. Which animal would you choose? Write a conversation that takes place between the two of you.

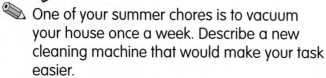

August 25

✎ One of your summer chores is to vacuum your house once a week. Describe a new cleaning machine that would make your task easier.

✎ Which fairy-tale character would you most like to be? Explain.

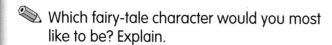

August 26

✎ Imagine that you have won a trip on the first passenger shuttle to Mars. List the advantages and disadvantages of making the journey.

✎ Pretend that you are the first news reporter to arrive at the scene of some breaking news. Write a short story to report this event to the public.

August 27

✎ Imagine that you dive into a pool to cool off and then realize that the pool has no bottom. Describe what you see and where you end up as you explore the pool.

✎ What is the one item you think all students should have when heading back to school? Explain.

August 28

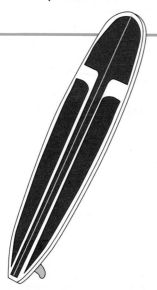

✎ Imagine that you are taking your brand-new surfboard into the ocean for the first time. As you are paddling out to catch the waves, you realize that your surfboard has special powers. Write about your experiences with your magic surfboard.

✎ It's almost time to meet your new teacher for the upcoming school year. Write a letter to your teacher about what you hope to learn in his or her class this year.

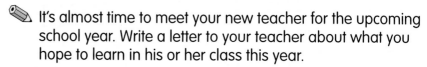

10

August 29

 Write a story that begins with the sentence "I knew it wasn't going to be my day when the wind blew away my homework."

 Pretend that you're a monkey in the zoo and you spot some children eating a banana. Explain what you would do to get their attention and persuade them to give you the banana.

August 30

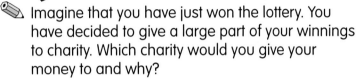 Imagine that you have just won the lottery. You have decided to give a large part of your winnings to charity. Which charity would you give your money to and why?

 After getting ready for school, you sit down for a quick breakfast. You pour yourself a bowl of cereal and pick up your spoon to eat when you notice something wiggling around in the bowl. Write about what happens next.

August 31

 Imagine that you are in science class preparing to start an experiment. Your teacher says, "For this experiment you must wear your safety goggles." Describe the experiment and what happens when you conduct it.

 Pretend that a toy company has just challenged you to create the ultimate new toy that every child will beg for. Describe your new creation and give it a name.

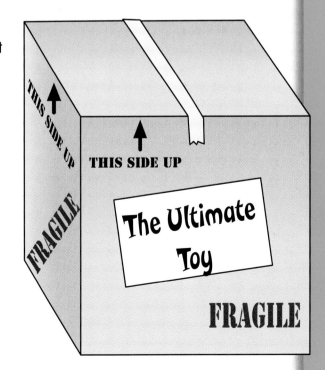

THIS SIDE UP

THIS SIDE UP

FRAGILE

The Ultimate Toy

FRAGILE

AUGUST

S E P T E M B E R

September 1

✏ National Waffle Week is celebrated the first week in September. Who said that waffles are just for breakfast! Describe how to incorporate waffles into a meal for lunch or dinner. Be sure to name your newly created meal.

✏ Write about your favorite or least favorite first-day-of-school memory.

SEPTEMBER						
S	M	T	W	T	F	S
				1	2	3
4	5	6	7	8	9	10
11	12	13	14	15	16	17
18	19	20	21	22	23	24
25	26	27	28	29	30	

September 2

✏ Labor Day is held on the first Monday in September. Name three occupations that you think are very important. Explain.

✏ For many people, Labor Day signals the end of summer. Does the end of summer make you happy or sad? Explain.

September 3

✏ Backpack Safety America Month is celebrated in September to remind students, parents, and teachers about the importance of packing and carrying a backpack safely. Describe a new way to safely carry your books and supplies to and from school.

✏ Imagine that as you are emptying your backpack at school, you find something soft and furry inside. Write about what happens next.

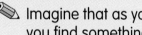

please

September 4

✏ September is Children's Good Manners Month. Describe a situation where someone is using poor manners. Then describe the same situation, only this time with someone using good manners.

thank you

✏ If you had to choose between having a computer or a television, which would you choose? Explain.

excuse me

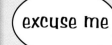

September 5

✎ Imagine that you are playing a video game with a friend when the two of you are pulled into the television and become part of the game. Write about what happens next.

✎ Describe a new hat that is perfect to wear for the fall season.

September 6

✎ September is National Honey Month. Write a paragraph describing honey.

✎ Pretend that you are a bear and you have just spotted a beehive dripping with honey. Describe how you will get the honey without being stung by the bees.

September 7

✎ Think of something that you could do to earn spending money. Write an advertisement for your business.

✎ Imagine that your parent put you in charge of doing the grocery shopping this week. What five items will you be sure to buy? Explain.

Grocery List

1.
2.
3.
4.
5.

September 8

You need me!

LIBRARY CARD

✎ What new subject would you like to add to your school day? Explain.

✎ September is Library Card Sign-Up Month. Create a top ten list of reasons to get a library card.

September 9

✎ September is National Very Important Parents (VIP) Month. Describe something that you could do to make your parent feel very important.

✎ Pretend that you are an ant and you spot a mushroom while out walking. Describe how it looks to you and how it can be useful to you.

September 10

✎ Which would you rather receive: The Nobel Peace Prize, an Academy Award, or the title of Most Valuable Player in the Super Bowl? Explain.

✎ Imagine that your school board is considering starting school an hour earlier. Write a letter to your school board expressing your opinion about this.

September 11

✎ Imagine that you have been selected to choose your new school mascot. What would you choose? Explain why this is a good choice for your school.

✎ If you could relive one school year all over again, which grade would you choose? Explain.

September 12

✎ National Grandparents Day is celebrated on the first Sunday after Labor Day. Would you prefer to have grown up during the time when your grandparents did? Explain.

✎ September 12 is Video Games Day. Imagine that you have been asked to come up with a concept for a new video game. Describe it.

September 13

✎ Children's author Roald Dahl was born on September 13, 1916. In his book *Charlie and the Chocolate Factory,* Willy Wonka creates some very unusual candies. Imagine that you have been asked to create a new candy. Describe how it looks and tastes.

✎ Pretend that you just opened a fortune cookie and pulled out a very unusual fortune. Write about what happens next.

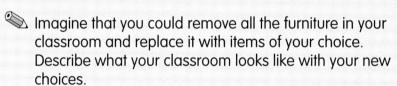

Substitute Survival Tips

1. _____
_____
2. _____
_____
3. _____
_____
4. _____
_____
5. _____

September 14

✎ Substitute Teacher Appreciation Week is celebrated the second week of September. Describe five of more characteristics of a good substitute teacher.

✎ Pretend that your teacher has asked you to compile a list of tips to help your next substitute teacher. What five tips would you include on the list?

September 15

✎ Family game night? Bedtime stories? Describe your favorite family tradition or a family tradition that you would like to start.

✎ Imagine that you could remove all the furniture in your classroom and replace it with items of your choice. Describe what your classroom looks like with your new choices.

September 16

✎ On this day in 1620, 102 passengers left England aboard the *Mayflower*. They landed at Plymouth, Massachusetts, on December 26, 1620. Imagine that your family decides to leave your home to go live in another country. Describe how you feel about leaving home forever.

✎ Imagine that you are a teacher. Explain what you would do to make sure that students always complete their schoolwork.

S
E
P
T
E
M
B
E
R

September 17

✎ September 17 is Citizenship Day. Describe three qualities of a good citizen.

✎ Imagine that you've just been named the class movie critic. Write a review about a movie that you have recently seen. Would you recommend it to others?

September 18

✎ Would you rather cross the United States in a helicopter or a hot-air balloon? Explain.

✎ Imagine that you are a bird and can fly over any location or event. Where or what would you like to fly over? Explain

September 19

✎ What one book from the library should every child your age read? Explain.

✎ The third full week in September is National Farm Animals Awareness Week. If you could be any animal that lives on a farm, which would you choose? Explain.

National Farm Animals Awareness Week

September 20

✎ Write a paragraph that starts with "I was outside jumping on my trampoline when all of a sudden…"

✎ Would you rather be president of the United States or the owner of a sports team? Explain.

September 21

✏ Imagine that you are making a guest appearance on your favorite television show. Describe what your day on the set is like and the role that you play.

✏ Would you rather be a shark or a whale? Explain.

September 22

✏ Today marks the anniversary of the ice-cream cone patent. Describe a new way of eating ice cream that does not involve a cone or a dish.

✏ Imagine that NASA has decided to take one school-age child into space on its next mission. Write a letter explaining why you should be chosen.

September 23

✏ September is National Homeschool Month. List three advantages and three disadvantages of homeschooling.

✏ Fall is here! Write a poem that tells about what you like or dislike about fall.

REPORT CARD	Wow!
English	A
Science	A
Math	A
History	A
Art	A
PE	A

September 24

✏ National School Success Month is celebrated in September. What advice would you give other students for how to be successful in school?

✏ If you had to spend an entire day in one room of your house, which room would you choose? Explain.

September 25

✏ The last full week in September is National Dog Week. Imagine that you are opening a dog spa where owners can bring their dogs to be pampered. Describe three activities that you will offer at your spa.

✏ Would your rather start school in the morning and finish in the afternoon or start school in the afternoon and finish in the evening? Explain.

September 26

✏ Today is Johnny Appleseed's birthday. He traveled around planting apple seeds in hopes of having a land with blossoming apple trees and no one hungry. If you could travel across the country helping people, what one thing would you do? Explain.

✏ Imagine that your PE teacher is out for the day and you are in charge of the class. What activity would you plan to be sure that everyone has fun and still gets exercise? Explain.

September 27

✏ Imagine that one day you left something in your classroom and that night the custodian of your school unlocks the doors of the school to let you get it. As you walk down the hall, you see a strange light coming from the library. Write about what happens next.

✏ Name three or more colors that remind you of fall. Explain.

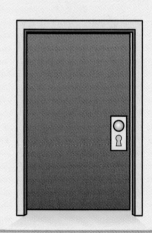

September 28

✏ Imagine that you take a sip of your friend's drink and something strange begins to happen. Write about what happens next.

✏ Pretend that you are a dog that belongs to the president of the United States. Describe your typical day.

September 29

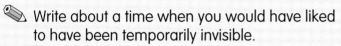 Imagine that you are digging in the dirt when your fingers run across something cold and slimy. Describe what you have found.

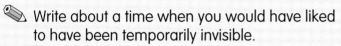 Write about a time when you would have liked to have been temporarily invisible.

September 30

 Would you rather relive the month of September over again, or are you looking forward to the month of October? Explain.

 *The Flintstones* premiered on this day in 1960. This cartoon was set in prehistoric times. Do you think you would have wanted to live when dinosaurs walked the earth? Explain.

October 1

✏️ The CD player was introduced on this day in 1982. Name a CD that you plan to have in your collection for years to come. Explain.

✏️ World Smile Day is the first Friday in October. Describe three or more things you have done recently that made someone smile.

October 2

✏️ October is National Cookie Month. What is your favorite kind of cookie? Explain.

✏️ Pretend you are a scarecrow and you are about to retire from your post. Write some advice for the rookie taking your place.

October 3

✏️ The first full week in October is National Newspaper Week. Write a letter to the editor of your local newspaper stating whether or not kids should have an assigned bedtime. Support your opinion with reasons.

✏️ Compare this year's school experiences to last year's. How are they alike? How are they different?

October 4

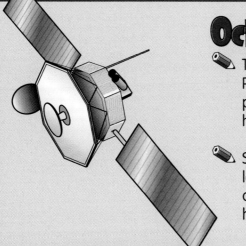

✏️ The first Monday in October is Child Health Day. Pretend you are a newborn baby. Write a letter to your parents explaining what they should do to keep you healthy and safe as you grow up.

✏️ Sputnik, the world's first man-made satellite, was launched on October 4, 1957. What space travel first do you think will happen in your lifetime? Describe how it will affect life on Earth.

October 5

✎ Name three qualities that you think are important for a teacher to have. Explain.

✎ Imagine that you are walking through a park. Suddenly a squirrel approaches you and asks for directions to the best place for storing nuts. Write about the conversation that takes place between you and the squirrel.

October 6

✎ The first full week in October is Get Organized Week. Rate how organized you are on a scale of one (not organized at all) to ten (extremely organized). Then describe how you can become organized, or explain how you stay organized.

✎ Imagine that one fall day you wake up to find that leaves are turning blue and purple instead of the typical fall colors. Write a paragraph explaining why this is happening.

October 7

✎ October is National Dental Hygiene Month. Write a paragraph for the Tooth Fairy Handbook that explains what the tooth fairy should do with all the teeth she collects during this month.

✎ Pretend you are a leaf changing colors. Write a paragraph describing how you feel.

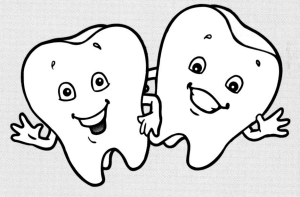

October 8

✎ The second Friday in October is World Egg Day. Celebrate by writing a humorous paragraph involving eggs.

✎ If you could write a best-selling book, what would it be about? Write a paragraph for the book jacket that describes what your book is about.

October 9

✎ Fire Prevention Week is celebrated in October. Write a paragraph convincing someone to install fire detectors and to check them regularly.

✎ October is National Roller Skating Month. Imagine that you find a card tucked in a pair of skates that says "To scale the sides of buildings, touch your nose. To fly, tug your ear." Write about what happens next.

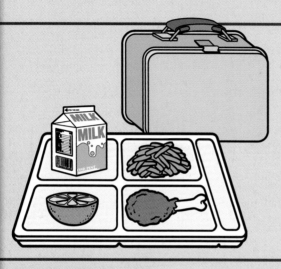

October 10

✎ National School Lunch Week starts on the second Sunday in October. Describe your favorite school lunch.

✎ Write a radio commercial to attract kids to a costume store. Include information about the store's stock, service, location, and hours.

October 11

✎ Columbus Day is celebrated on the second Monday in October. Do you think it will still be celebrated 200 years from now? Explain.

✎ Today is Eleanor Roosevelt's birthday. Mrs. Roosevelt once said, "The future belongs to those who believe in the beauty of their dreams." Describe a dream that you have for the future.

October 12

✎ In honor of Computer Learning Month, write directions explaining how to win at your favorite computer game.

✎ Write about a time when you saved the day.

October 13

✏️ October is Adopt-a-Shelter-Dog Month. Write ten tips to help a person select the perfect canine companion.

✏️ What are your goals for this school year? How will you accomplish them? How will you overcome any obstacles that get in your way?

You're Invited
_____
_____
_____

October 14

✏️ October is Eat Better, Eat Together Month. Write an invitation to a friend or a family member to join you for a meal. Include details about when you'll meet and what you'll eat.

✏️ Pretend that your town is considering banning trick-or-treating because it disturbs some residents. Write a letter to the council offering a solution that will please everyone.

October 15

✏️ October 15 is National Grouch Day. Make a list of animals that would like to celebrate this day. Explain why you selected each.

✏️ Write a paragraph that starts with the sentence "The craziest things happened to me at the library today."

October 16

✏️ Today is Dictionary Day in honor of Noah Webster's birthday. Name four or more words that describe you. Explain why you chose each word.

✏️ If you were asked to judge a pumpkin-carving contest, what guidelines would you use to select a winner?

October 17

✏️ October is National Stamp Collecting Month. Imagine that 50 years from now, a stamp will be created that honors you and your contributions to the world. Write a press release that tells the stamp's cost, describes the stamp's image, and outlines your accomplishments.

✏️ If you could permanently trade places with someone, whom would you choose? Explain.

October 18

✏️ Thomas Edison died on this day in 1931. He was a famous inventor who invented the lightbulb, the phonograph, and many other things. If you could ask Thomas Edison five questions, what would they be? Why?

✏️ The expression "blind as a bat" is false because bats can see about as well as humans can. Explain how you think this expression came about.

October 19

✏️ What is the first gift you remember receiving? Who gave it, what did it mean to you, and what happened to it?

✏️ Write a paragraph that ends with the sentence "I hope never to be that frightened again!"

October 20

✏️ You have been asked to star in a scary movie. After reading the script, you realize that some of the scenes will be very frightening to viewers. Would you still accept the role? Explain.

✏️ Many popular books have been made into movies. What book have you read that would make a good movie? Explain.

October 21

✏ October is Vegetarian Month. Create a new recipe that does not contain meat. List the ingredients and explain how to prepare it.

✏ You have been given a magic broomstick that will take you anywhere. Describe the places you travel to in a single night and how each place makes you feel.

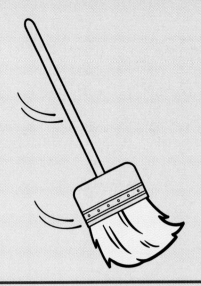

October 22

✏ October is National Animal Safety and Protection Month. Write a conversation between a stray dog and a dog inside a fenced yard.

✏ Imagine that a giant has just knocked on your door and demanded to be fed. Write directions for preparing a feast fit for a 50-foot giant.

Tink

October 23

✏ Pretend that you just found your favorite book character's diary. Write about the first entry.

✏ If you could host a TV talk show, who would you select to be on the first show? Explain.

Dear Mr. Boyd,
    I don't think we should have homework anymore.

October 24

✏ Today is United Nations Day. The United Nations works to promote human rights for all people. Make a list of basic human rights you believe all people should have. Explain.

✏ Imagine that you could change one thing about your school. Write a letter to your principal persuading her or him to make the change.

October 25

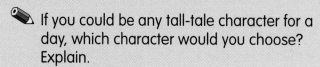

✎ Rank the months of the year in order from your most favorite to least favorite. Explain why you chose this order.

✎ If you could be any tall-tale character for a day, which character would you choose? Explain.

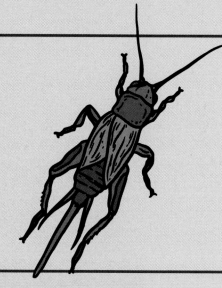

October 26

✎ Write a paragraph using the five senses to describe how you know that fall has arrived.

✎ Imagine that you are eating with your family in a fancy restaurant. You look down at your food and see a bug in it. Explain how you would handle the situation.

October 27

✎ The last week in October is Peace, Friendship and Good Will Week. Describe a program you can start that will help bring peace, friendship, and goodwill to your community or school.

✎ You've just been hired as the spokesperson for an amusement park. Your first job is to record a radio commercial for a ride. Choose a ride and write a radio commercial to persuade people to visit the park to ride it.

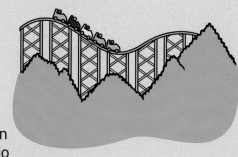

October 28

✎ Jonas Salk was born on this day in 1914. Salk developed a vaccine for polio. If you could develop a vaccine to prevent a disease, which disease would it be? Explain how your work would impact the nation and the world.

✎ If you could have a candy product named after you, what would it be? Describe the treat and why it should be named after you.

October 29

✏️ October is National Popcorn Poppin' Month. Imagine being the only kernel of popcorn that does not pop in a package. Describe how you feel about it.

✏️ Develop a plan to prove or disprove the existence of Bigfoot or the Loch Ness monster.

October 30

✏️ Imagine you are in a costume shop and one of the costumes suddenly comes to life! Write about what happens next.

✏️ Describe a meal or snack that hits the spot after a long, tiring day.

October 31

✏️ Should there be school on Halloween? Defend your opinion in a paragraph.

✏️ If you could get only one type of treat while trick-or-treating, what would it be? Explain.

November 1

✎ November 1 is National Authors' Day. Pretend that you are a famous author visiting an elementary school with a copy of your latest book. Write about how the children react when they meet you and see your new book.

✎ Today is National Family Literacy Day. List as many ways as you can that families can read and write together.

November 2

✎ November is Aviation History Month. Imagine that you just realized that you can fly. Write about how you discovered this new ability.

✎ The first seven days in November make up World Communication Week. Imagine that you could not use a television, a telephone, a cell phone, or a computer for an entire week. What would be the most difficult thing about the week? The easiest? Explain.

November 3

✎ November 3 is Sandwich Day. Create a unique sandwich in honor of someone you know. Give it a creative name and then describe how to make it.

✎ If you had to choose one holiday to not celebrate this year, which would you choose? Explain.

Charlie's Cheesed to Please

November 4

✎ Pretend that you have just created a drink that adds 15 years to a person's life. Describe what happens as you take the first sip.

✎ A common saying is "Home is where the heart is." Describe what you love about the town or city in which you live.

November 5

✎ Benjamin Franklin thought that the turkey would make a better national bird than the bald eagle. How might Thanksgiving be different if a turkey was the national bird of the United States? Explain.

✎ What invention do you hope will be created in your lifetime? Explain.

November 6

✎ Imagine that you could live anywhere in the world. Where would you live? Explain.

✎ The winter holiday season is right around the corner. Describe the perfect way to celebrate.

November 7

✎ Imagine that as you are shopping for a turkey for your Thanksgiving meal, a turkey walks by and says, "Put that down and buy a chicken instead." Write about what happens next.

✎ Would you like to be a famous athlete or a movie star? Explain.

MOVIE STAR

November 8

✎ Imagine that when you opened your classroom door, you saw your parent as the substitute teacher for the day. Describe your day at school.

✎ The X ray was discovered on this day in 1895. Pretend that you are a doctor examining a patient's X ray and see something very bizarre! Write about what happens next.

NOVEMBER

November 9

✏️ Pretend that you have been selected to ask the next presidential candidates five questions at an upcoming debate. List the five questions that you would ask and explain why each answer is important.

✏️ November is I Am So Thankful Month. List ten or more things for which you are thankful.

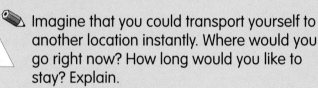

I Am So Thankful
1.
2.
3.
4.
5.
6.
7.
8.
9.
10.

November 10

✏️ Would a turkey make a good pet? Explain.

✏️ Imagine that you could transport yourself to another location instantly. Where would you go right now? How long would you like to stay? Explain.

November 11

✏️ Veterans Day is celebrated on November 11. Write the words for a new greeting card designed to be given to a veteran.

✏️ Imagine that while you are doing your homework, the words are disappearing as soon as you write them. Write about what happens next.

November 12

BACKROAD BOYS
SUMMER SUPER CONCERT
ROW 102   SEAT 3

✏️ Pretend that you just won free tickets to your favorite musical artist's concert. The problem is if you go to the concert, you will miss your best friend's birthday party. Explain what you would do.

✏️ If you could invite ten people to attend a special dinner, whom would you choose? Explain.

November 13

✏️ Today is World Kindness Day. To celebrate, write the letters of your name in a column and write an acrostic poem that describes ways that you can be kind to others.

✏️ Imagine that you just opened a cereal box to find that the prize inside looks nothing like the advertisement you saw on television. Write a letter to the company explaining how you feel.

C ‎
O ‎
L ‎
E ‎

November 14

✏️ William Steig, author of the book *Shrek!*, was born on November 14. Imagine that a story you wrote is being made into a movie. Write a radio ad encouraging people to see the movie.

✏️ Today is National American Teddy Bear Day. Write about what happens after you find your teddy bear sitting at your desk doing your homework.

November 15

✏️ Today is America Recycles Day. Imagine that you've just invented a machine that recycles a common everyday item by turning it into something fabulous. Write about what your machine recycles and what the item becomes.

✏️ Pretend that your teacher is moving away and your principal has asked you to write a help wanted ad for a new teacher. What would your ad say?

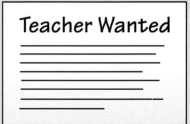

Teacher Wanted

November 16

✏️ Would you rather have a week of 90°F days or a week of snowy days? Explain.

✏️ Imagine that you are mistakenly locked inside a factory that makes your favorite food and you aren't found for several days. Explain how you feel after being discovered.

November 17

✎ If you could invite one person to come to your classroom for a day, who would it be? Why would you pick this person?

✎ The day before Thanksgiving is What Do You Love About America Day. Write a top ten list featuring your favorite things about the country. Explain why you included each one.

November 18

✎ The Great American Smokeout is held each November. Write a pledge in which you promise to never smoke. In the pledge, give three or more reasons for not smoking.

✎ November 18 is Mickey Mouse's birthday. Describe how you imagine this day being celebrated at Walt Disney World.

November 19

✎ November 19 is Have a Bad Day Day. Imagine that four things have happened today to make it a really bad day. Write about your day using the words *first*, *then*, *next*, and *finally*.

✎ Children's Book Week is celebrated in November. What three books would you recommend for a younger child to read in order to trigger a love for reading? Explain.

November 20

✎ Create special awards to honor each member of your family, including yourself. Explain each award.

✎ November 20 is Name Your PC Day. What name would you give a new PC? Explain.

November 21

✎ If you could only eat two foods for your Thanksgiving meal, which two would you choose? Explain.

✎ Today is World Hello Day. Imagine that you have been asked to select a word to replace *hello*. Which word would you choose? Explain.

November 22

✎ Write about the perfect Thanksgiving Day.

✎ Imagine that your parent told your sister that she could have any pet that she wanted. Describe your family's new outrageous pet and what it is like living with it.

November 23

✎ The week of Thanksgiving is National Game and Puzzle Week. Would you rather play a game or work a puzzle? Explain.

✎ Are you more like a tree in fall or a tree in winter? Explain.

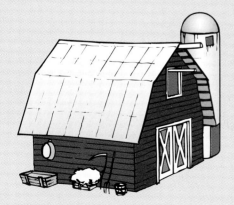

November 24

✎ Imagine that you have just received an email message from a classmate saying that she has found $100. She wants you to meet her in the town park to share the money. Explain what you would do.

✎ Would you rather live and work on a farm or live and work in the city? Explain.

November 25

✏️ Pretend that the power has gone out just as your family is preparing to cook Thanksgiving dinner. Create an alternative menu that requires no cooking.

✏️ Which would you rather watch on television: a football game or a Thanksgiving Day parade? Explain.

BIG SALE

November 26

✏️ The Friday after Thanksgiving is a popular shopping day. Pretend that you are out shopping for gifts for your family. What gift would you buy for each of your family members if money was no object? Explain.

✏️ Are you most thankful for the things you've done, the places you've been, or the people you've known? Explain.

HAPPY THANKSGIVING

November 27

✏️ What do you like most about the month of November? Least? Explain.

✏️ Write a letter to the organizers of the Macy's Thanksgiving Day Parade requesting that they bring the event to your town next year.

November 28

✏️ Imagine that your family has been invited to dinner by your new neighbors. When dinner is served, you cannot believe your eyes. Write about what happens next.

✏️ Write a letter persuading lawmakers to pass either a law that requires leftovers to be served at least twice a week or a law that bans leftovers from being served.

NOVEMBER

November 29

✎ Today is Electronic Greetings Day. Write a conversation that you might overhear between a computer and a paper greeting card.

✎ Would you rather know how to play an instrument well or draw well? Explain.

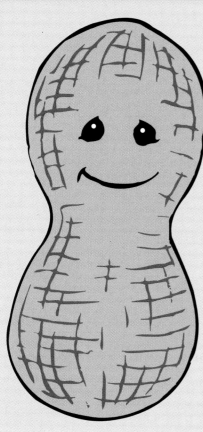

November 30

✎ Today is the last day of Peanut Butter Lovers' Month. Pretend that you are a peanut. Are you happy or sad to see the month end? Explain.

✎ What three adjectives would you use to describe your best friend? Explain.

December 1

✏️ Basketball was created on December 1, 1891. Imagine that you are playing for your favorite team, and all of the fans are cheering for you. Describe how you feel.

✏️ December is bingo's birthday month. Invent a new and improved version of bingo that you and your friends would enjoy playing. Be sure to include directions so others can play.

December 2

✏️ The first week in December is National Cookie Cutter Week. Imagine that you have been invited to participate in a cookie-baking contest. Describe five unusual cookie cutter shapes that would be sure to make your cookies stand out.

✏️ You've just heard a report on the evening news that all businesses are going to be closed the entire month of December due to bad weather. How will people in your community need to prepare for this?

December 3

✏️ December is National Tie Month. Ties come in all shapes, sizes, and colors. Design a tie for someone special. Describe what it looks like.

✏️ December is a month of giving, and each person has unique gifts and talents to share! Tell about a talent you have and how you could give it as a gift to someone.

December 4

✏️ The month of December can be quite chilly in parts of the country. Imagine that today the temperature is well below freezing. Write five similes describing what you feel like. Example: It's so cold today that I feel like an ice pop in a freezer!

✏️ Your parents have taken you to the circus. During a performance, you sneak behind the big top. Describe what happens next.

December 5

✏️ Imagine that a mysterious nutcracker suddenly begins to whisper a message to you. You look around the room, and no one else seems to notice. Write about what the nutcracker is saying to you.

✏️ December is National Stress-Free Family Holidays Month. Make a list of things you can do for your teacher, family, and friends that will make December less stressful for them.

Help needed for Santa's workshop

December 6

✏️ Imagine that one cold, dark evening, as you are curling up by the fire with a cup of hot cocoa and a good book, you hear a strange noise outside of your house. Do you go and investigate, or do you hide under a blanket? Explain what happens next.

✏️ Pretend that you open today's newspaper and find a help wanted ad for Santa's workshop. Write Santa a letter convincing him to hire you to work in his workshop.

December 7

✏️ Holiday decorations are all over this time of year! If you could decorate your home any way that you liked, what would you do? Explain.

✏️ Walking home from school one snowy day, you see a reindeer propped up against a barn, reading! Write about what happens next.

December 8

✏️ During Hanukkah, Jewish families light a candle and give each other gifts for eight consecutive nights. Make a list of eight gifts you could give someone in your family that would not cost any money.

✏️ Pretend that one evening your aunt and uncle give you a baby polar bear as a gift! Do you think it will make a good pet? Explain why or why not.

DECEMBER

December 9

✎ Pretend that one morning you and your family awaken to discover that you are snowed in! You are trapped inside all day. Explain what you will do together to pass the time.

✎ Make a list of ten things you could do to help a person or group in your community.

WELCOME TO SUMMER CAMP

December 10

✎ Pretend that you have been asked to create a new holiday candy. Describe the new candy using your five senses.

✎ Summer may be six months away, but December is National Sign Up for Summer Camp Month. Describe the type of camp you would like to sign up for and the activities in which you would most like to participate.

December 11

✎ What color reminds you of cold winter weather? What color makes you think about warm summer weather? Which of the two colors do you like better? Explain.

✎ Imagine that you hear the sound of jingling bells off in the distance. The bells seem to be getting closer and closer. Write about what happens next.

December 12

✎ Imagine that you wake up in the middle of the night to find a sack of gifts at the foot of your bed. You reach inside the sack and pull out the perfect gift. Describe the gift.

✎ Poinsettias are flowering plants that are popular around this time of year. Make a list of other items that are generally only found this time of year.

December 13

✏️ Imagine that a card company has asked you to design a holiday card. What would your card look like, and what would it say? Explain.

✏️ A is for airplane, and B is for bicycle. Write your own toy alphabet from A to Z.

December 14

✏️ Imagine that while everyone was sleeping last night, an elf came into your classroom. Why did he come? What did he do? Describe what happened to your classroom.

✏️ Imagine that you are buying a holiday gift for a friend and the store clerk gives you too much change back. Explain what you would do.

December 15

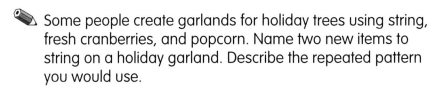

✏️ On December 15 we celebrate the Bill of Rights. What right do you not have that you think you should have? Explain.

✏️ Some people create garlands for holiday trees using string, fresh cranberries, and popcorn. Name two new items to string on a holiday garland. Describe the repeated pattern you would use.

Things to do:

8:30–9:30 Watch cartoons

9:30–11:00 _____

11:00–12:00 _____

12:00–12:30 _____

12:30–4:00 _____

4:00–6:00 _____

6:00–9:30 _____

December 16

✏️ Pretend that you are a Christmas tree, and it is the week before Christmas. What do you see going on around you? How do you feel? Explain.

✏️ You wake up to a snow-covered ground and learn school is closed. Write a schedule showing what you will do this day. Be sure to include the times you will start and finish each activity.

D
E
C
E
M
B
E
R

December 17

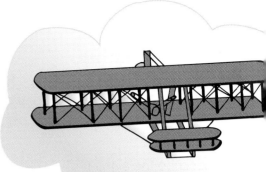

✏️ From an adult's perspective, describe what the perfect holiday would be.

✏️ Pretend that it is December 17, 2121. The Wright brothers would have flown their first airplane 218 years ago. Write a letter to the brothers describing what air travel is like in this year.

December 18

✏️ Pretend that you wake up one morning during Christmas vacation to discover that the rest of your family left for a trip without you. Write about what happens next.

✏️ This year is almost over. Make a list of five things that you did well this past year. Then list five things you hope to accomplish next year.

December 19

✏️ Create a new family tradition for celebrating the holidays. Explain what would make this tradition so special to your family.

✏️ Imagine that you are a pioneer living on the prairie. Describe what your life is like this time of year.

December 20

✏️ The third Friday in December is Underdog Day. Write about a time you or someone you know was an underdog.

✏️ Make a list of all the gifts you could give that cost one dollar or less. Then tell whom you would give them to.

December 21

✏️ World Peace Day is celebrated today. Think of someone whom you do not get along with. What can you do to make peace with that person? Explain.

✏️ Describe the signs that mean that Old Man Winter has arrived.

December 22

✏️ The movie *Snow White and the Seven Dwarfs* premiered in December 1937. List seven important people in your life. Explain.

✏️ Imagine that Santa has asked your class for help. He needs 50 gifts wrapped in 15 minutes. Describe the best way to get the job done.

December 23

✏️ Pretend that you wake up to find you have turned into a reindeer! Tomorrow is Christmas Eve. Write about what happens next.

✏️ Pretend that your younger brother has never wrapped a present before. Help him out by writing directions for wrapping a boxed gift.

December 24

✏️ Imagine that it's Christmas Eve and you find a jolly stranger sitting in a chair, eating cookies and drinking milk. He says hello, and you begin to talk. Write about your conversation.

✏️ Describe the sounds you might hear outside your bedroom window on a clear, cool night.

DECEMBER

December 25

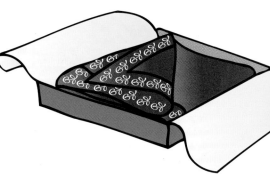

✏️ Imagine that your family has decided to make each others' gifts this year. Describe what you would make for each of your family members.

✏️ Pretend that you open a gift and find a red bandana. Describe at least five different ways you could use it.

December 26

✏️ Today is the first day of Kwanzaa. During Kwanzaa, families light green candles that represent hope. What are your hopes for the future?

✏️ Today is National Whiner's Day. Write five things you would like to whine and complain about. For each item listed, write one thing you could do about it instead of whining.

December 27

✏️ Giving thanks is an important part of the holidays. Write ten different ways to thank someone.

✏️ Name an animal with a unique feature, such as a giraffe or a zebra. Make up a story explaining how the animal got that feature.

December 28

✏️ Pretend that you are living on the sun. Write a forecast for today's weather.

✏️ Imagine that you open a magazine and find you have become an overnight star! What is your talent? How did you develop your skill? What is the first thing you will do as a celebrity?

December 29

✎ Imagine that you are the runaway gingerbread man. What are you running to? Explain.

✎ The YMCA was organized on this day. Pretend that you have been asked to give a speech on the importance of health and fitness to your class. What would you say?

December 30

✎ Today is No Interruptions Day! Who do you think will enjoy this day more: your parent or your teacher? Explain.

✎ Pretend that you come home from school and receive a written message from your pet. Describe what the note says and what happens next.

December 31

✎ Today is Make Up Your Mind Day. Think about the toughest decision you have ever had to make. Did you make the right choice? Explain why or why not.

✎ On New Year's Eve, many people make resolutions for the upcoming year but fail to keep them. Write one resolution you have. Then write a reminder note encouraging yourself to keep your resolution.

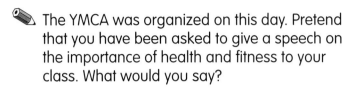

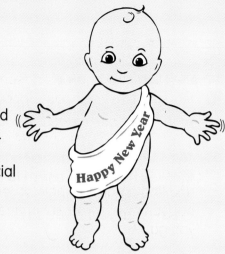

January 1

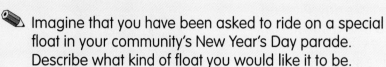

✎ Write about a resolution you wish you had made and kept last year that would have made the year better.

✎ Imagine that you have been asked to ride on a special float in your community's New Year's Day parade. Describe what kind of float you would like it to be.

January 2

✎ Pretend that you and your family are taking a cruise this month. Where will you go? What items will you pack in your suitcases?

✎ Mittens, twins, and salt and pepper shakers come in twos. What other things come in twos?

January 3

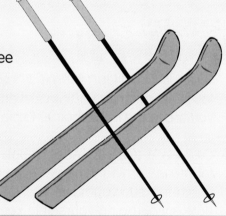

✎ January is Family Fit Lifestyle Month. Describe three activities that your family could do together three times each week to help each member be more physically fit.

✎ Would you rather go skiing or snowboarding? Explain.

January 4

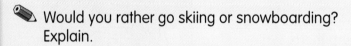

✎ Imagine that as you are drinking a cup of hot cocoa, it suddenly shouts, "Stop! Please don't drink me!" Write about what happens next.

✎ *Snowflake* is a compound word. Write five more compound words that include the word *snow*. Use three of the words to help you write a poem about winter.

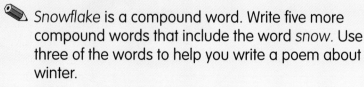

January 5

✏ Describe how you would rearrange or redecorate any room in your house. Include a sentence about each area in the room that you change. Tell why you are making the change.

✏ Pretend that you are walking in your neighborhood and find a pair of magic shoes. Write about what happens when you put on the shoes and where you go.

January 6

✏ Think of a time in your life when something happened to you that you did not expect. Write about that time and how you felt.

✏ If a cold January wind could talk, what do you think it would say to trees? To buildings? To animals? To people?

January 7

✏ Imagine that all field trips have been canceled for the year. Write a letter to your principal explaining your opinion about this. Include three reasons to support your opinion.

✏ How could a white rabbit hide itself in the winter if there were no snow? Write a paragraph to explain your thoughts.

January 8

✏ Write a paragraph explaining what you think the following saying means: "Don't count your chickens before they hatch."

✏ If you could eat one of the following fruits, which would you pick: a plum, an apple, an orange, or grapes? Explain.

January 9

✏️ Some say that the best things in life are free. Do you agree with this? Explain.

✏️ Pretend that the town council wants to create a billboard advertising your community. List ten reasons why your community is a great place to live.

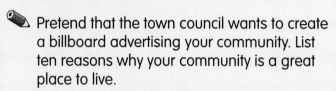

FREE!

January 10

✏️ Explain what you would do if you were playing inside your house one snowy Saturday and found a trail of strange, wet footprints leading from your front door to your attic.

✏️ Which of the following words describes you best: *curious, sensitive, outspoken, accident-prone?* Explain.

January 11

✏️ Imagine that you have just won a special award. Write an acceptance speech that includes what the award is for.

✏️ Describe an animal that can be seen outside at this time of year.

BEST SPELLER

Here's how I want my things arranged.

January 12

✏️ Write a note from your desk to you. In the note, have the desk explain how it would like the things inside it to be arranged.

✏️ Pretend that you open the morning paper and find a want ad for a responsible student. Write what the ad might say.

January 13

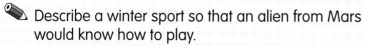

✏️ Pretend that a new friend will spend Friday evening with you and your family. Write directions from school to your house so the friend will know how to get there.

✏️ Describe a winter sport so that an alien from Mars would know how to play.

January 14

✏️ Describe what your life would be like if you were a book in the library.

✏️ Surprise! A family member just drove up in a new vehicle! Tell what kind of vehicle it is. Then give five reasons why the purchase was made.

January 15

✏️ Martin Luther King Jr. was born on this day in 1929. He believed in equal rights for all people. Explain what having equal rights means.

✏️ Imagine that when the mail comes today, there is a package for you. Describe what you would like to find in the package.

January 16

✏️ Would you enjoy having a day with nothing to do? Explain.

✏️ Pretend that you are a reporter who has been sent back in time to cover an important event in history. Write a brief news story about the event. Include the five Ws: who, what, when, where, and why.

January 17

✏ Benjamin Franklin was born on this day in 1706. He once flew a kite during a thunderstorm to prove that lightning is a form of electricity. Was this a wise thing to do? Explain.

✏ Describe how even a small child can show courage.

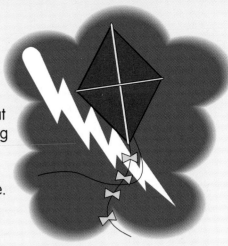

January 18

STAR BATTLE
6:15 Showing
PALLADIUM THEATER

STAR BATTLE
6:15 Showing
PALLADIUM THEATER

✏ A. A. Milne, the author of *Winnie-the-Pooh*, was born on this day in 1882. If you could be one of this book's characters, would you prefer to be Pooh, Piglet, Tigger, or Eeyore? Explain.

✏ Pretend that your best friend has invited you to the movies. You really want to go, but you promised your grandmother you would spend the afternoon with her. Write about what you decide to do.

January 19

✏ The tin can was patented on this day in 1825. Today tin cans are recycled. Describe five things you could do to get someone who is not recycling cans to start doing so now.

✏ What would you do if you found out that your best friend had not kept the secret you had asked him or her not to tell?

January 20

✏ Suppose you are walking through a snowy forest and can understand what two deer are saying to each other. Write the conversation you hear.

✏ Pretend it is a gray, cloudy day. Describe three things you could do that you would not be able to do if it were a clear, sunny day.

January 21

- In honor of Squirrel Appreciation Day, list as many foods as you can that contain nuts. Then explain how you would convince your mom or dad to make one of the foods for dinner tonight.

- After eating an afternoon snack of popcorn, you find that you can no longer sit down anywhere without popping out of your chair! Explain what you finally do to get back to normal.

January 22

- Today is Answer Your Cat's Question Day. Pretend that you see your cat sitting at your computer. It has typed three questions. What are they? How will you answer each question?

- Pick one of the following jobs and explain why this job is important to the community: firefighter, police officer, or mayor.

January 23

- Today is National Handwriting Day. Write a note to your doctor explaining why it is so important that he or she always write neatly.

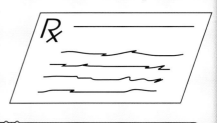

- Pretend that you write an advice column for your school newspaper. What advice would you give a new student who is having problems making friends?

January 24

- Imagine that by accident you get locked in a department store after it closes for the night. Describe how you spend the night.

- Wow! You are going to be a guest on a talk show for kids! What will you talk about? Why?

January 25

Pretend that your school building has feelings like a real person. When school is closed because of snow, do you think the building feels happy or sad? Why?

Your morning got off to an interesting start. As you began to eat your breakfast cereal, it talked to you! What did it say?

January 26

January is Walk Your Pet Month. Besides walking your pet daily, explain five other important things you should do to care for it.

Write the directions for playing your favorite indoor game in five easy steps.

January 27

Cool! You have just created a delicious new flavor of ice cream! Write a letter to persuade your favorite ice-cream shop to sell your creation. In your letter, include four reasons why your ice cream will be a top seller.

Explain how to set your dinner table for a regular family meal.

Crunchy Caramel Popcorn Ice Cream

January 28

Winter can be a difficult time for outdoor animals. Pretend that a squirrel has asked you for ideas about how to make its home all cozy and warm. What will you suggest?

If your pencil could talk, what do you think it would say about being pushed around on paper to form letters, numbers, and punctuation marks? Explain.

January 29

✏️ You've just spotted a wise old owl sitting in a tree. If the owl could talk, what three things do you think it would say to you?

✏️ How are a bicycle, a car, and a scooter alike? Different?

January 30

✏️ Today is Fun at Work Day. Write a note to your parent suggesting five zany things he or she could do to have fun at work.

✏️ Pretend that you have a substitute teacher today. Imagine that every time she scratches her nose, all of the books in the classroom begin acting strangely. Write about what happens when she scratches her nose and then sneezes.

January 31

✏️ What would your family rather do together: go bowling, see a movie, play a board game, or have an indoor picnic? Explain.

✏️ Uh-oh! A winter storm warning has just been issued for your area. Describe what you and your family will do to prepare for it.

A winter storm warning is in effect.

JANUARY

FEBRUARY

February 1

✏️ Jerry Spinelli, author of the Newbery Award winner *Maniac Magee*, was born on February 1. In this story, a boy is given the nickname Maniac Magee. Give yourself a nickname. Explain why you chose this name.

✏️ Pretend that you and your family are entering a family baking contest. What would you and your family bake? Explain why your family's baked item should be the winning entry.

February 2

✏️ February 2 is Groundhog Day. In the wild, groundhogs eat plants such as grass, alfalfa, and clover. Imagine that this year on Groundhog Day, the groundhog came out of his hole and requested a meal of human food. What would you serve him? Explain.

✏️ Imagine that you live underground like a groundhog. Describe what your house looks like.

February 3

✏️ Elizabeth Blackwell was born on February 3, 1821. She was the first woman physician. If you were a doctor, what type would you be? Pediatrician? Foot doctor? Surgeon? Other? Explain.

✏️ Today is the anniversary of the coldest recorded temperature in North America. On February 3, 1947, it was 81 degrees below zero in Canada's Yukon Territory. Would you rather be too cold or too hot? Explain.

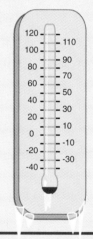

February 4

✏️ Imagine that you just got your pilot's license and can fly anywhere in the world. Where would you fly first? Explain.

✏️ What one thing would you like to do for a family member or friend to make his or her life better? Explain.

February 5

✏ February 5 is Weatherperson's Day. Pretend that you are a weatherperson reporting on a weather-related breaking news story. Write what you would be broadcasting.

✏ Think about a time when you have worked as part of a team. Write about this experience.

February 6

✏ What one compliment would you like to give your best friend? Explain.

✏ Pretend that you are a squirrel. Describe how you feel after a huge snowfall.

February 7

✏ Laura Ingalls Wilder was born on February 7, 1867. She wrote many books about growing up as a young pioneer. Imagine that you have no electricity or running water. Write about a day in your life without these luxuries.

✏ Imagine that a pioneer girl arrives at your school in a time machine. Name three things that you think would surprise her. Explain.

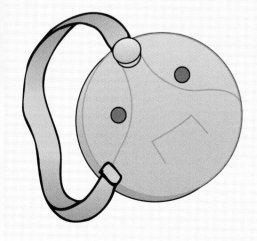

February 8

✏ Imagine that you and your family are on a camping trip in a remote wilderness area when most of your gear falls over a cliff. You are left with only a pocket knife and a canteen of water. Explain what you would do to survive for four days.

✏ Would you rather go white-water rafting or skiing? Explain.

February 9

✎ February is National Children's Dental Health Month. Write the words to a short song that encourages children to brush their teeth every day.

✎ Pretend that your teacher has asked you to teach a lesson on table manners to a kindergarten class in your school. Write five dos and five don'ts that you can share with them.

February 10

✎ February is Black History Month. Think of a famous Black American author, singer, athlete, or TV personality. Write a letter congratulating this person on his or her accomplishments.

✎ Imagine that you had to eat chocolate with every meal this month. Would this be a good thing or a bad thing? Explain.

February 11

✎ Thomas Edison, inventor of the lightbulb, was born on February 11, 1847. List as many items as you can that use lightbulbs. Then write about how life would be different without this important invention.

✎ Imagine that you have a little brother and he just lost his first tooth. Other than money, what would you like the Tooth Fairy to leave him under his pillow.

February 12

✎ Today is Lost Penny Day, a day set aside to put all those pennies stashed in jars, candy dishes, and drawers back into circulation. Imagine that your class collected all its lost pennies to donate to a charity. Which charity would you donate them to? Explain.

✎ Would you rather eat a hot breakfast or a cold breakfast? Explain.

February 13

✐ Would you rather receive a box of chocolates, flowers, or a book for Valentine's Day? Explain.

✐ Select one classroom object. Write a paragraph describing the object without naming it.

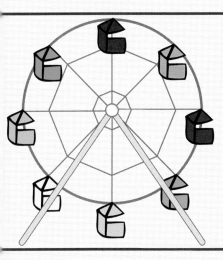

February 14

✐ Today is Valentine's Day. Imagine that you have just anonymously received the perfect gift. Write about what it is and how you will figure out who gave it to you.

✐ February 14 is Ferris Wheel Day in honor of George Washington Gale Ferris, the engineer who invented the Ferris wheel. Would you rather ride a Ferris wheel or a roller coaster? Explain.

February 15

✐ February is Library Lovers' Month. Write a top ten list of reasons to love the library.

✐ Imagine that your friend has just come to you very upset after failing a math test. Explain what you would tell your friend to help make him or her feel better.

February 16

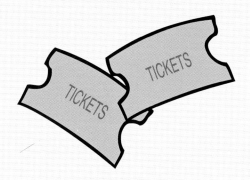

✐ The third Monday in February is Presidents' Day. Would you rather be president of the United States or a famous movie star? Explain.

✐ Describe the sights and sounds of an amusement park or a carnival.

February 17

✎ Imagine that you are president of your elementary school. What would you do to try to improve your school and make students happier?

✎ Pretend that you are a fish that has just been caught. What would you say to the person who caught you to convince him or her to let you go?

February 18

✎ On this date in 1930 the planet Pluto was discovered by astronomer Clyde Tombaugh. Pretend that you are an astronomer who just discovered another planet in our solar system. Name your planet and describe what it looks like and where it is located.

✎ Imagine that you find a pair of magical slippers that allow you to travel anywhere in the world and to any time period past or present. Where would you go and what time period would you choose? Explain.

February 19

✎ Would you rather go scuba diving or skydiving? Explain.

✎ Imagine that you are a cat and a huge dog is chasing you. Write about what you would do to outwit the dog and make your way to safety.

February 20

✎ Imagine that you just won the lottery, but you must share your earnings with another person. With whom would you share? Explain.

✎ Pretend that you just found a ladder that leads into the ground. Write about what happens next.

February 21

YAWN

✎ Imagine that you are the captain of your own ship. Where would you sail to? Who would travel with you? Explain.

✎ Pretend that you have just received from a friend a letter that had been lost in the mail for a month. Write about your letter's month-long adventure.

February 22

✎ National Pancake Week is celebrated in February. Create a recipe for a pancake sandwich that uses two pancakes in place of bread. What will you call your sandwich creation?

✎ The first president of the United States, George Washington, was born on February 22, 1732. Imagine that you pull a dollar out of your pocket and the picture of George Washington begins to talk to you. Write about the conversation that you have with him.

February 23

✎ Would you rather have six months of winter or six months of summer? Explain.

✎ Imagine that you are a tree. What would you say to the neighborhood children to convince them to come hang out on your branches?

February 24

✎ International Friendship Week is celebrated the last full week in February. Imagine that you could be penpals with a child from any country in the world. Which country would you choose? Explain.

✎ When sharing a project with the class, would you rather present first or last? Explain.

February 25

✎ Think of your favorite book. Imagine that you are a new character entering the story. What type of character would you be, and how would your character change the story?

✎ Explain what you would do if you discovered that one of your classmates cheated on a test.

February 26

✎ Imagine that you are a shark and all the other fish in the sea are afraid of you. What would you say to convince them that you are really friendly?

✎ Write a poem that describes how you feel about winter.

February 27

✎ Imagine that you are a hockey puck during a hockey game. Describe how you feel.

✎ Would you rather be wearing jeans and a sweatshirt or shorts and a T-shirt? Explain.

February 28

✎ Imagine that you could be a guest actor on any TV show. What show would you choose, and what would you like your role to be?

✎ Explain what you would do if you found out your best friend lied to you about something.

February 29

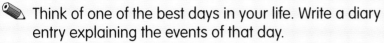 Imagine that you were born on February 29, which is only on the calendar every fourth year. What day would you choose to celebrate your birthday the other years? Explain.

 Think of one of the best days in your life. Write a diary entry explaining the events of that day.

Dear Diary, Today was the best day of my life! It all started...

March 1

✎ Newspaper in Education week is observed in March. Pretend you are an editor for the local newspaper. Write an article about something exciting happening in your school.

✎ Today is National Pig Day. Imagine you wake up one morning to discover that you have grown a pink snout and a curly tail. Write about what happens next.

March 2

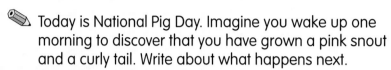

✎ March is Music in Our Schools Month. Pretend you could only communicate by playing instruments instead of talking or gesturing. What instrument would you use? Explain.

✎ March is National Craft Month. Pretend your assignment is to explain to a first-grade class how to make your favorite craft. What would you teach them to make, and why do you think they would like it?

March 3

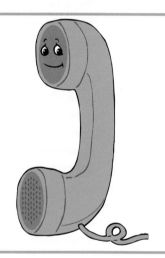

✎ Today is National Anthem Day. Describe how you feel when you hear our national anthem being played.

✎ Alexander Graham Bell was born on March 3, 1847. Write about what your life would be like without the telephone.

March 4

✎ Think about what makes you happier than anything else in the world. Describe how others can join in and be happy too.

✎ It's never too early to start saving for college. List several ways you could earn money for college.

M
A
R
C
H

March 5

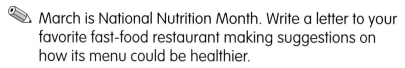

✎ Celebrate Your Name Week is observed the first full week in March. Write a fictional story explaining how you got your name.

✎ March is National Nutrition Month. Write a letter to your favorite fast-food restaurant making suggestions on how its menu could be healthier.

Dear McBurger's Fast Food,

March 6

✎ Would rather be a polar bear or a grizzly bear? Explain.

✎ Imagine that dogs and cats have thumbs. With this new addition, what would be different about having a dog or cat as a pet? Explain.

March 7

✎ Imagine you are an animal living on a farm or in a zoo. Describe what your everyday life would be like.

✎ The game Monopoly was invented on this day in 1933. Imagine that the Parker Brothers Company has asked you to design a new version of the game. Describe what you would change.

March 8

✎ March is Save Your Vision Month. Imagine that you could have the eyesight of any animal. Which animal would you choose? Explain.

✎ Pretend that you can travel back in time and change one thing in your life. What would you change and why?

MARCH

March 9

✎ Imagine you and a friend are in a race for a million dollars. In the middle of the race, your friend falls and breaks her ankle. Do you continue on in the race, leaving your friend behind, or do you stop to help? Explain.

✎ Pretend you have magical powers and could go anywhere in the world and do anything. Where would you go, and what would you do? Explain.

March 10

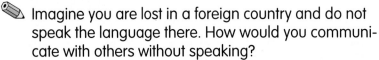

✎ The first U.S. paper money was issued on this day in 1862. If we did not use money as currency, what could be used in its place? Explain.

✎ Would you rather live in a place that experiences hurricanes or tornadoes? Explain.

March 11

✎ Imagine you are lost in a foreign country and do not speak the language there. How would you communicate with others without speaking?

✎ Imagine that you found a package of magic seeds that can grow anything you wish. What would you grow? Explain.

MAGIC SEEDS

March 12

✎ The Girl Scouts of the USA was founded on this day in 1912. Design an advertisement to convince girls to join this organization.

✎ Some very powerful people wear hats, such as generals, kings, and queens. If you could wear someone else's hat and become him or her for a day, whose hat would you choose? Explain.

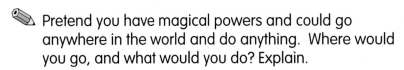

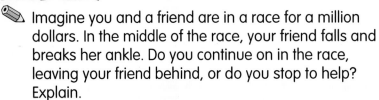

March 13

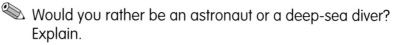 Would you rather be an astronaut or a deep-sea diver? Explain.

Today is National Open an Umbrella Indoors Day. Some people say that this is bad luck. Do you believe in bad luck? Explain.

March 14

After waiting all winter, what is your favorite thing to do once spring arrives? Explain.

Write a paragraph that starts "It was a very windy day...."

REPORT CARD	
English	F
Science	B
Math	B
History	B
Art	A
PE	A

March 15

Imagine you just failed a test that you needed a good grade on in order to pass the class. Would you tell your parent about the grade right away, or would you wait until report cards were sent home? Explain.

If you could fast-forward or rewind to any age, what age would you be? Explain.

March 16

Imagine that you wake up and discover that everything you touch turns green. Write about what happens next.

The U.S. Military Academy was founded on this day in 1802. Their motto is "Duty, Honor, Country." If you had to create your own motto to live by, what would it be? Explain.

March 17

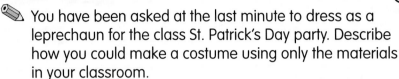
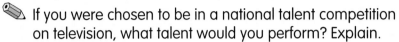

✎ You have been asked at the last minute to dress as a leprechaun for the class St. Patrick's Day party. Describe how you could make a costume using only the materials in your classroom.

✎ If you were chosen to be in a national talent competition on television, what talent would you perform? Explain.

March 18

✎ Describe your most awkward moment and how you felt at the time.

✎ Imagine you find Jack's beanstalk and climb it. At the top you spot the castle and decide to explore. Once inside, the giant notices you. Write about what happens next.

March 19

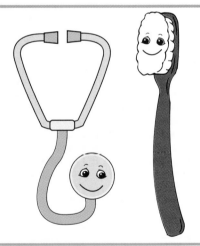

✎ If you could remake your favorite movie, which one would you choose and what would you change?

✎ Would you rather go to the doctor or the dentist? Explain.

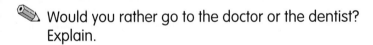

March 20

✎ The first day of spring is also National Agriculture Day. Describe something unique that you and your classmates could plant in your schoolyard for students to enjoy now and in the future. Use your imagination.

✎ Think of a favorite television show that you watched when you were younger. What was it called? Why did you like to watch it?

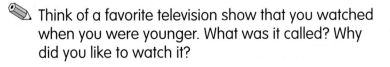

M A R C H

64

March 21

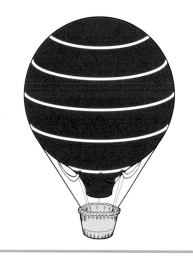

✎ The first round-the-world balloon flight happened on this day in 1999. If you had the opportunity to travel and see the world from a hot-air balloon, would you? Explain.

✎ Imagine that you have been hired to create a new cereal that can be eaten for breakfast, lunch, and dinner. Describe what you would create.

March 22

✎ What advice would you give someone so that he or she would have an upbeat and positive outlook on life?

✎ Would you rather be a lion or a lamb? Explain.

March 23

✎ If you and your family were stranded on a desert island, list ten things you would want to have with you that do not require electricity.

✎ Pretend that you are the richest person in the world. Describe one day in your life.

March 24

✎ Imagine that you and your family are on vacation at your favorite summer spot. Would you rather sleep in and relax or wake up early to go exploring? Explain.

✎ Imagine that during a sleepover your friend tells you that she is scared because she thinks there is a monster in her closet. What would you do to help calm her down and make her feel safe?

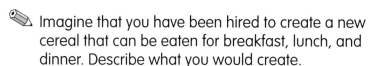

March 25

✎ Think about the student who might be sitting in your classroom chair next year. What can he or she expect from your teacher and the year to come?

✎ Pretend that you can put on a special coat and become invisible. Where would you go, and what would you do?

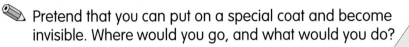

March 26

✎ Music can be relaxing and can bring back good memories. What are some of your favorite songs, and how do they make you feel?

✎ Today is Make Up Your Own Holiday Day. Describe a holiday that you would create and explain how you would get others to observe and participate in your holiday.

March 27

✎ Patty Smith Hill, the author of the lyrics to "Happy Birthday to You," was born on this day in 1868. In honor of her birthday, create a new version of her song.

✎ The last week in March is National Cleaning Week. Describe what your house or school might look like if no one ever cleaned it.

March 28

✎ On March 28, 1881, the Barnum and Bailey Circus was formed to create the "Greatest Show on Earth." How do you feel about people using wild animals for entertainment? Explain.

✎ Explain what "The early bird catches the worm" means to you.

March 29

✎ Would you rather stay up late and sleep late in the morning, or would you rather go to bed early and wake up early? Explain.

✎ April Fools' Day is rapidly approaching. Do you feel that students should be able to play jokes or pull pranks at school on this day? Explain.

March 30

✎ Today is Doctors' Day. Imagine and describe what the world would be like without doctors.

✎ On this day in 1858 the first pencil with an eraser top was patented. Draw and describe a new and improved pencil that you think other students might like.

March 31

✎ Pretend you are a talk show host. Name several people whom you would like to interview. What would you talk about?

✎ What TV show family is most like your family? What are the similarities and differences? Explain.

MARCH

April 1

✏️ Today is April Fools' Day. Would you rather play a joke on someone or have a joke played on you? Explain.

✏️ Pretend that you are a raindrop. Describe what you see and do on your adventure through the water cycle.

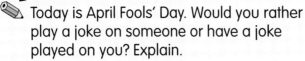

April 2

✏️ Nickelodeon, the cable TV channel for kids, debuted on this date in 1979. Imagine that you have been asked to create the next new television show for the network. Describe what your show would be about and what would make it successful.

✏️ April 2 is International Children's Book Day. Pretend that you are a children's book that has been sitting on a library shelf for weeks without being checked out. What would you say to convince someone to check you out?

April 3

✏️ April is National Humor Month. Imagine what life would be like if everyone in the world were always serious. Do you think this would be a positive thing? Explain.

✏️ Pretend that you are an earthworm crawling through the ground when suddenly a rain shower begins to soak the ground. Write about what happens next.

April 4

✏️ April is National Kite Month. Pretend that you are a kite. Write a weather report for a perfect day for you.

✏️ List ten or more things that you can do indoors on a rainy day. Circle your favorite and give reasons for your selection.

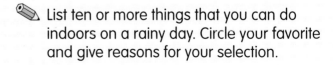

April 5

✎ What is a hobby you have or would like to have? Explain what you like most about it.

✎ Pretend that you are a bulb lying dormant underground. The warm April sun is causing you to emerge to the surface. Describe what it feels like to grow, bloom, and then wither away.

April 6

✎ Imagine that your town has just made it mandatory for every child to participate on a sports team. Is this a good thing? Explain.

✎ Describe your perfect spring break.

April 7

✎ Imagine that you have just won the Build a Better Umbrella contest. Describe the new and improved umbrella design that won you the contest.

✎ Would you rather be a bird or an insect? Explain.

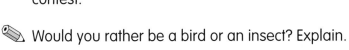

April 8

✎ National Soft Pretzel Month is in April. Write a silly paragraph explaining how pretzels came to be shaped the way they are.

✎ Describe the funniest thing you've seen or heard this month.

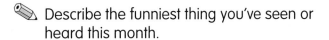

April 9

✎ April is National Poetry Month. Use the letters in the word *spring* to write an acrostic poem about spring.

✎ Do you think thunderstorms are scary or cool? Explain.

S _____
P _____
R _____
I _____
N _____
G _____

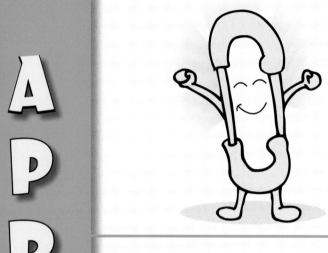

April 10

✎ National Siblings Day is April 10. Would you rather be an only child or have siblings? Explain.

✎ The safety pin was patented on April 10, 1849. Write a story that ends with "That little safety pin saved the day!"

April 11

✎ Pretend that you are working in the garden when you find the most unusual thing. Write about what happens next.

✎ Would you rather be a vegetable plant or a flower? Explain.

April 12

✎ Author Beverly Cleary was born on April 12. She wrote many popular books, including *Dear Mr. Henshaw, Strider, The Mouse and the Motorcycle,* and the Ramona series. Write five or more questions that you would ask Beverly Cleary if you got the chance to meet her.

✎ Are you more like a hard-boiled egg or a scrambled egg? Explain.

A P R I L

April 13

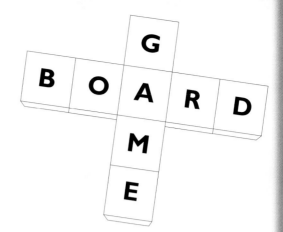

✏️ Alfred M. Butts, inventor of the board game Scrabble, was born on this day in 1899. Write instructions on how to play your favorite board game.

✏️ Combine the features of two different insects to create a new insect. Name and describe your new creature.

April 14

✏️ Write about how Easter celebrations and decorations might be different if instead of an Easter Bunny, there were an Easter Frog.

✏️ What is your favorite recess game or activity? Explain.

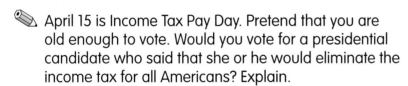

A
P
R
I
L

April 15

✏️ April is Prevention of Animal Cruelty Month. Write a letter to the editor of your local newspaper expressing your thoughts on animal cruelty.

✏️ April 15 is Income Tax Pay Day. Pretend that you are old enough to vote. Would you vote for a presidential candidate who said that she or he would eliminate the income tax for all Americans? Explain.

APRIL
15
Taxes Due

April 16

✏️ National Wear Your Pajamas to Work Day is held each year the day after income taxes are due. Why do you think it is held on this day? When would be a good time to have a National Wear Your Pajamas to School Day? Explain.

✏️ What new school rule would you like to implement? How would this new rule make your school a better place?

April 17

✏ Imagine that you are walking through the park with your friend and you find a bag of money. Explain what you would do.

✏ List five or more things that you and your family can do to help the environment.

April 18

✏ National Coin Week is celebrated in April. Pretend that coin money will no longer be used in the United States. Explain how everyday life might be different.

✏ Baseball? Piano? Dancing? What one afterschool activity would you like to participate in? Write a letter to your parent to persuade him or her to let you participate.

April 19

✏ National Library Week is celebrated in April. Write a note to your best friend explaining why you should meet at the library instead of the playground today.

✏ National TV-Turnoff Week is held in April. Pretend that you are celebrating it by not turning your TV on all week. When you turn the TV back on again, what is the first thing you'd want to watch? Explain.

April 20

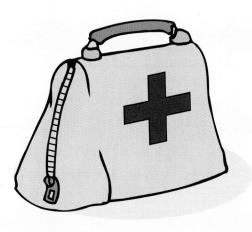

✏ Pretend that the Great Games company has asked you to design a new board game. Describe the game and how it is played.

✏ Would you rather be a professional athlete or a doctor? Explain.

April 21

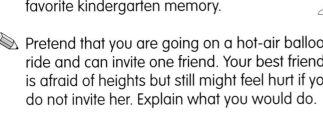

April 21 is Kindergarten Day. Describe your favorite kindergarten memory.

Pretend that you are going on a hot-air balloon ride and can invite one friend. Your best friend is afraid of heights but still might feel hurt if you do not invite her. Explain what you would do.

April 22

"A penny saved is a penny earned" are famous words of Benjamin Franklin. What do you think he meant? Do you agree?

The fourth Thursday in April is Take Our Daughters and Sons to Work Day. Would you like to have a Bring Your Parent to School Day? Explain.

April 23

The first movie theater opened in New York City on April 23, 1896. Would you rather watch your favorite movie at the theater or at your own house? Explain.

The first public school in America opened on this day in 1635. How do you think the first day of school in 1635 would compare to your first day of school this year?

April 24

List as many words as you can that rhyme with *spring*. Use the list to create the message for a greeting card that wishes someone a happy spring.

Imagine that you could take a trip to any planet in our solar system. Which planet would you most like to visit? Which planet would you least like to visit? Explain.

April 25

✏️ On this date in 1901, New York became the first state to require license plates on vehicles. Using no more than eight letters or numbers, design a personalized license plate for yourself. Explain what it means and why you chose it.

✏️ Every 2½ minutes, a child requires emergency-room treatment for a playground-related injury. Pick one kind of playground equipment, such as a swing or a slide, and redesign it to be safer. Describe your new design.

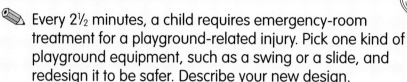

April 26

✏️ April 26 is Richter Scale Day. This scale measures the magnitude of an earthquake. The higher the number, the stronger the quake is. Number your paper one to five. List five things that personally shake you up. The higher the number, the more it shakes you up.

✏️ Imagine that you are flying a kite when suddenly you are lifted up and start soaring with the kite. Write about what happens next.

April 27

✏️ Pretend that you can redecorate your best friend's bedroom any way you want. Describe what your new room looks like.

✏️ Would you rather be an ant at a picnic or a bee in a flower garden? Explain.

April 28

✏️ Pretend that you are a bird. Write the steps for building the perfect nest.

✏️ Are you more like a spring thunderstorm or a winter snowstorm? Explain.

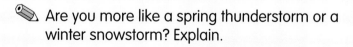

April 29

✎ The zipper was patented on April 29, 1913. Imagine that you are camping in the woods with a friend. As you try to get out of the tent in the morning, you realize that the zipper is stuck. Write about what happens next.

✎ The last Friday in April is National Arbor Day. Write a letter to your school council convincing them to plant 15 new trees outside your school.

April 30

✎ April 30 is National Honesty Day. Do you think that there is ever a time when it is okay to be dishonest? Explain.

✎ April showers are said to bring May flowers. Pretend that you are a flower. Write a thank-you note to the rain showers.

May 1

 May 1 is Mother Goose Day. Choose two nursery rhyme characters, such as Little Miss Muffet, Old Mother Hubbard, Humpty Dumpty, or Little Boy Blue. Write about an encounter between these two characters.

 School Principals' Day is May 1. Pretend that your school will no longer have a principal. Write about how things might be different.

May 2

 The first full week in May is Be Kind to Animals Week. Write a poem or a paragraph that expresses the importance of animals in your life.

 If you were a flower, would you rather be planted in a garden at someone's house or at a park? Explain.

May 3

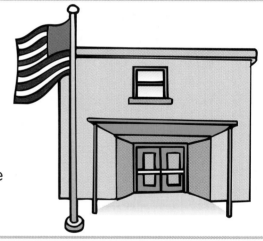

 The first full week in May is National Family Week. What is your favorite way to spend time with family? Explain.

 Imagine that you arrive at school one day and there are no teachers or any other adults in the building. Write about what happens next.

Top Ten Reasons to Honor Teachers
_____
_____
_____
_____
_____
_____
_____
_____
_____
_____
_____
_____

May 4

 National Teacher Day is celebrated on the Tuesday of the first full week in May. Create a top ten list giving reasons why we should honor teachers with a special day.

 Imagine that when you get home from school one day, your family looks different and they are acting very strange. Write about what happens next.

M
A
Y

May 5

 May is National Book Month. Would you rather read more books or fewer books than you currently read? Explain.

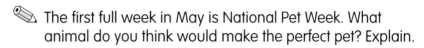 The first full week in May is National Pet Week. What animal do you think would make the perfect pet? Explain.

May 6

✐ What would you say to your teacher to convince him or her to allow you to have one night a week without homework?

✐ Imagine that you woke up this morning to find that you had grown springs on your feet. Write about one day with this new addition to your feet.

May 7

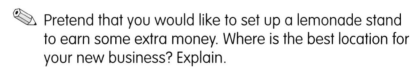 Imagine that you are an animal living in the wild. What animal are you, and what is your favorite time of the year? Explain.

✐ Pretend that you would like to set up a lemonade stand to earn some extra money. Where is the best location for your new business? Explain.

May 8

✐ The Saturday before Mother's Day is National Babysitters Day. Imagine that you are with a babysitter when a storm knocks out the power. Write about what happens next.

✐ May 8 is No Socks Day. Pretend that you are a sock. Describe how you will spend your day off duty.

May 9

✎ The second Sunday in May is Mother's Day. Write a paragraph describing your definition of a mother.

✎ Would you rather visit a friend's house or have a friend visit your house? Explain.

May 10

✎ May is National Egg Month. Write a mouth-watering description of a new way to enjoy eggs.

✎ Imagine that you had to spend an entire day outside. Write about how you would spend your day.

May 11

✎ Write a letter to yourself explaining why it is important to participate in some type of physical fitness activity or sport.

✎ Write a silly paragraph explaining how leopards came to have spots.

May 12

✎ National Bike Month is celebrated in May. Explain how life would be different if you had to ride a bicycle to get around.

✎ Would you rather go on a safari in Africa or visit a rain forest in Central America? Explain.

M A Y

May 13

✎ If you could play any professional sport, what would you play? Explain.

✎ Pretend that your parent has asked you to give up one type of junk food and eat a healthy food in its place for a month. What food would you give up? What would you replace it with? Explain.

May 14

✎ Imagine that your family is preparing for a garage sale to get rid of any unwanted household items. Your parent has told you that you must select at least three items from your room to sell. What three items would you sell? Explain.

✎ Pretend that you are shopping at a garage sale when suddenly you hear a toy doll speaking to you. Write about what happens next.

Hey there!

May 15

✎ National Etiquette Week is celebrated the third week in May. Write five or more rules that you think should be included in a book called "Using Your Manners at School."

✎ Would you rather be a police officer or a firefighter? Explain.

May 16

✎ National Transportation Week is celebrated the week that includes the third Friday in May. In what ways do you think transportation will be different 25 years from now? In what ways do you think it will be the same?

✎ Would you rather be a caterpillar or a butterfly? Explain.

M A Y

MAY

May 17

✐ The author of *Hatchet*, Gary Paulsen, was born on May 17. In *Hatchet*, a boy is the only survivor of a small plane crash in the Canadian wilderness. Imagine that this was you. What five items would you like to have with you? Explain.

✐ Write about a time when you tried something new.

May 18

✐ Today is International Museum Day. Imagine that you have to live in a museum as a caretaker. Which museum would you like to live in? Explain.

✐ Pretend that money does grow on trees. How might life be different?

May 19

✐ May 19 is Visit Your Relatives Day. Which relative would you most like to visit? Explain how you would spend your day.

✐ Pretend that you are a young scientist receiving an award for your latest invention. Write a short article for a science magazine describing your new invention.

May 20

✐ Imagine that while on a field trip with your class, you discover something that has never been seen before. What do you find? Explain how you will tell the world about your discovery.

✐ May is National Physical Fitness and Sports Month. Write an exercise plan for yourself to implement over the next seven days. What will you do to stay active?

May 21

🖎 Is it ever okay to break a promise? Explain.

🖎 The third Friday in May is National Bike to Work Day. Not all people can safely ride a bike to work or school. Explain what you would do to make riding to work or school safer.

May 22

🖎 Pretend that you are a famous author of many award-winning books. What would you say to children about the importance of reading and writing?

🖎 Do you prefer to read books or magazines? Explain.

May 23

🖎 May is Young Achievers Month. Name one young person that you admire. Explain.

🖎 Young achievers probably had big dreams and high hopes. What do you dream about accomplishing someday? Explain.

May 24

🖎 May is National Older Americans Month. Write a letter to an elderly person in your life telling him or her how much he or she means to you.

🖎 Would you rather spend an hour playing a video game or playing a board game? Explain.

M
A
Y

May 25

 If you were a superhero, what special power would you like to have? Explain.

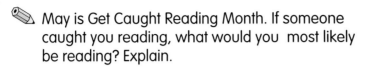 May is Get Caught Reading Month. If someone caught you reading, what would you most likely be reading? Explain.

 Dear Author,

May 26

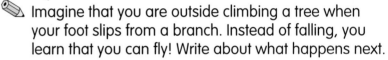 Imagine that you are outside climbing a tree when your foot slips from a branch. Instead of falling, you learn that you can fly! Write about what happens next.

Write a letter to the author of your favorite book explaining why you enjoyed it so much.

May 27

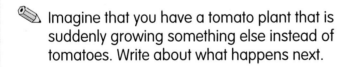 If you could change the color of your hair, would you? Explain.

Imagine that you have a tomato plant that is suddenly growing something else instead of tomatoes. Write about what happens next.

May 28

 Which book character would you like to have come to life? Explain.

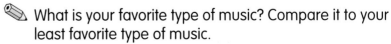 What is your favorite type of music? Compare it to your least favorite type of music.

May 29

✎ May is National Hamburger Month. What is your favorite food? Which month would you like to designate to honor this food? Explain.

✎ Imagine that you are a farmer and you just discovered that your hen is laying golden eggs. Write about what happens next.

March

Last Day of School

May 30

✎ What candy bar are you most like? Explain.

✎ Imagine that your state is planning to cut two months from your school calendar. Is this a good or bad thing? Explain.

May 31

✎ Pretend that you found a stray dog. Describe how you would attempt to find its owner.

✎ Imagine that today is Name Your Own Holiday Day. What would you name today? Explain.

June 1

✏️ Some students get the summer itch toward the end of the school year. Describe the symptoms of this ailment and what you would do to cure it.

✏️ As students get out of school for summer break, it is important for them to remember safety rules. Make a list of safety tips for students to follow during summer months.

June 2

✏️ Babe Ruth, one of the best hitters of all time, retired from baseball on this day in 1935. What is something that you would like to do better than anyone else? Explain.

✏️ Pretend that the company that makes M&M's candies has decided to add a new color to the bag. Write a letter to the company president telling him or her what color you think should be added and why.

June 3

✏️ Many kids head off to summer camp during the month of June. Create a packing list of items that kids would not want to forget when packing for camp.

✏️ Pretend that you are a zookeeper. Describe one day on the job.

June 4

✏️ Imagine that as you are walking home one afternoon, you find an injured animal lying on the ground. Describe what you would do next.

✏️ Summer is fun, but it also means summer chores. What is the one chore that you dislike the most? Explain.

June 5

✎ Would you rather play inside or outside in the summer? Explain.

✎ A Chinese proverb says, "Give a man a fish and you feed him for a day. Teach a man to fish and you feed him for a lifetime." Explain what you think this means.

June 6

✎ Imagine that you have just been elected president of your neighborhood kids' club. Describe what activities you will provide for the kids and how you will run the club.

✎ June is Fireworks Safety Month. Pretend that you are a firecracker. What would you say to children about fireworks safety?

June 7

✎ Imagine that you are at summer camp and have just finished the most exciting outdoor event of your life. Write a postcard describing this wild adventure to your family.

✎ On June 7, 1975, the Sony corporation sold the very first VCR for $995. How might life be different without video cameras and video recorders? Explain.

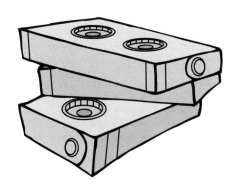

June 8

✎ Write a paragraph that starts with the sentence "I can't believe that we have to go to school all summer long."

✎ Imagine that you receive a phone call from your favorite celebrity. Who is calling you, and what do you talk about?

June 9

Today is Donald Duck's birthday. Imagine that the Walt Disney World theme park has decided to create a ride called Gone Quackers. Describe what the ride looks like and what kind of adventures await you.

Your family is going on vacation and will have to leave your pet (or a pet you would like to have) at home. Write out special instructions for the pet sitter on how to care for your pet.

June 10

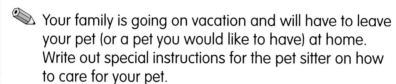

The ballpoint pen was patented on this day in 1943. Write a letter to your teacher persuading her to allow you to complete all of your work in pen instead of pencil.

Would you rather write in pen or pencil? Compare and contrast these two writing utensils and write about which one you prefer.

June 11

June is Dairy Month. Pretend your class is on a field trip to the local ice-cream factory when a conveyor belt goes out of control. Write about what happens next.

Chunky Monkey ice cream is an actual flavor made by Ben & Jerry's. Pretend the company has hired you to create a new flavor of ice cream. List the ingredients you would use and possible names for the new flavor.

June 12

It's Turkey Lover's Month. Imagine the circus has a singing-turkey act. Describe what can be seen and heard at the show.

Some people love turkey; others love steak. Some people can't get enough cookies, while others love cake. Write a poem about the food you wouldn't want to live without.

June 13

✏️ June is National Rose Month. Imagine you decide to "smell the roses" and take a walk through your favorite place. Describe the different scents in the air and how they make you feel.

✏️ On this day in 1884, the world's first roller-coaster ride opened. Describe the perfect theme park.

June 14

✏️ Today is Flag Day. What does saying the Pledge of Allegiance and saluting the flag mean to you?

✏️ Imagine that it is 1776 and Betsy Ross has asked you to help her design the American flag. What suggestions and changes would you make? Describe this new flag.

June 15

✏️ Describe your favorite place to go with family. What makes this place so special?

✏️ Would you rather walk outside barefoot or with shoes on? Explain.

June 16

✏️ If you were a skilled juggler, what kinds of objects would you like to try to juggle? Explain.

✏️ When people get very busy, it is said that they are juggling their schedules. What do you think would be a good saying for when you have lots of homework to finish? Explain.

June 17

 Imagine that your friend has had the hiccups for three days. He has tried everything to alleviate his problem, but nothing has worked. What would you suggest he do next?

 Australia is known as the land down under. What would be a good nickname for Antarctica and why?

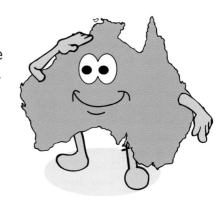

June 18

 Imagine that you and your family are taking a walk through the park when you notice a furry tail sticking out from under the bushes. You slowly reach down to touch it. Write about what happens next.

 June is a great time to play outside, ride bikes, or in-line skate. Compare two pieces of sporting equipment and write about which you prefer.

June 19

 Imagine that your family tells you that you are moving to another country in 24 hours. Make a list of everything you would want to do before leaving.

 Write a story that ends with the line "That's why I'll never eat another…"

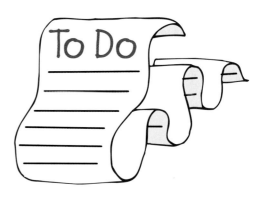

June 20

 Write about a lesson you learned by watching a movie or reading a book.

 Summer is almost here! Depending on where you live, you may be wearing shorts and a tank top, or even a swimsuit to stay cool. Describe your favorite summertime outfit.

June 21

✏ Because of the summer solstice, the sun will not set in areas near the Arctic Circle for several days. Describe what it might be like where it's constantly daytime and never night.

✏ Finish the following sentence with your most mind-boggling thought. "I just don't understand why…" Then give your best guess to answer the question.

June 22

✏ What is one thing that you hate to do, but you know you have to do it? Explain.

✏ Pretend that today is your birthday. Describe the perfect birthday party.

June 23

✏ Describe a time when you thought, "I should have listened to my parent (or teacher)."

✏ Pretend that you step up to the bowling lane and are about to let go of the bowling ball when you notice something moving around behind the pins. Write about what happens next.

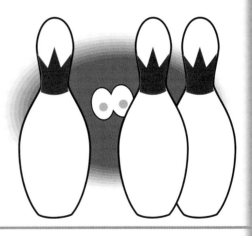

June 24

✏ Imagine that everyone is allowed to bring pets to school. Is this a good or bad idea? Explain.

✏ It's a hot summer day, and you are bored out of your mind. With just a Frisbee toy and two plastic cups, invent a game that you think would be a blast to play.

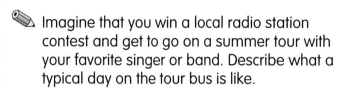

June 25

✏️ Pretend your parent surprises you one day and says that you can buy anything you want, but you can only shop in one store. What store would you choose, and what would you buy?

✏️ Imagine that you win a local radio station contest and get to go on a summer tour with your favorite singer or band. Describe what a typical day on the tour bus is like.

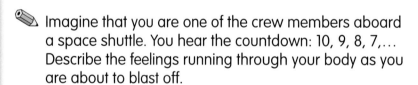

From:
The White House
1600 Pennsylvania Avenue
Washington, DC

To:
You

June 26

✏️ Pretend that you receive an envelope in the mail from the White House. What is in the envelope, and what do you do next?

✏️ Write a letter to the president of the United States telling him five things you think he could do to improve schools.

June 27

✏️ Imagine that your parents insist that you go to bed at 8:00 P.M. Write a letter to your parents persuading them to let you have a later bedtime during summer vacation.

✏️ Imagine that you are one of the crew members aboard a space shuttle. You hear the countdown: 10, 9, 8, 7,... Describe the feelings running through your body as you are about to blast off.

June 28

✏️ Some people are remembered for charity work. Others are remembered for being great entertainers. What would you like others to remember you for? Explain.

✏️ There are 186 more days left in this calendar year. Write a story problem using this information. Then write the steps explaining how to solve your problem.

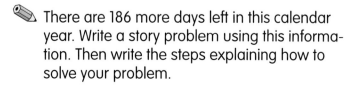

June 29

✏️ Summer is in full swing! List three things you would like to accomplish this summer before returning to school in the fall. Explain.

✏️ Imagine that shoes and feet can communicate with each other. Write a conversation that might take place between your foot and shoe as you are walking along the beach.

June 30

✏️ Imagine that you fall asleep while floating on a raft in the ocean. Write about what happens next.

✏️ On June 30, 1859, Charles Blondin walked across Niagara Falls on a tightrope. Imagine one of your friends wants to do something dangerous. What would you say to him? Explain.

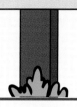

ZOO
Adults: $0.25
Children: $0.10

July 1

✎ The first U.S. zoo opened in Philadelphia on this day in 1874. Imagine that you are there on opening day. Describe what you see and how you feel.

✎ I Forgot Day is celebrated on the 183rd day of the year. Write a note to a friend or family member apologizing for something that you recently forgot.

July 2

✎ Design a parade float that features three or more symbols that represent what it means to be free in the United States. Describe the design of your float, explaining each featured symbol.

✎ What would fireworks say if they could talk? Write a conversation that might take place during a big celebration.

July 3

✎ Plan an itinerary of five or more things that you can do while staying out of the sun today.

✎ On a hot summer day, would you rather ride in a car with the windows down or with the windows up and the air conditioning turned on? Explain.

July 4

✎ Today is the birthday of the United States. If you could give our country any present that you can imagine, what would you choose? Explain.

✎ Imagine that while watching fireworks, you realize that the fireworks are spelling out messages that are directed at you! Write about what happens next.

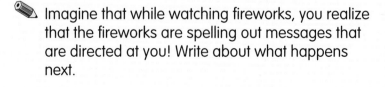

JULY

July 5

- The 26th amendment to the U.S. Constitution was proclaimed on this day in 1971. This amendment set the voting age at 18 years of age. Do you think this is an appropriate age to begin voting? Explain.

- Describe the sights, sounds, and smells of a summer night.

July 6

- What one thing would you like to accomplish by the end of the summer? Explain.

- Would you rather go swimming in a pool, a lake, or an ocean. Explain.

July 7

- What do you like most about summer? Least? Explain.

- Pretend that you got on a bus this morning headed for camp. When you arrived, you realized that you got on the wrong bus, and you are now at the wrong camp! Write about what happens next.

July 8

- Create a list of goofy things to do this summer. Will you teach your dog to whistle or build an ant farm for your cousin?

- Imagine that you applied a new sunscreen that goes on green but is supposed to fade. As you head for the pool, you are getting greener and greener. Write about what happens next.

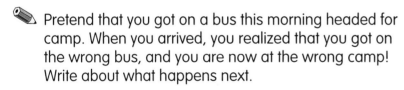

JULY

93

July 9

✏ Imagine that you have a choice of attending one of two exclusive summer camps. You can attend camp in the Florida Everglades or in the mountains of Colorado. Which camp would you choose? Explain.

✏ Describe your perfect summer day.

CAMP EVERGLADES

CAMP Colorado

July 10

✏ If you were a fish, would you rather live in a lake or a river? Explain.

✏ Imagine that you are starring in the lead role of this summer's blockbuster movie. Write about what your summer will be like.

July 11

✏ Imagine that your principal has decided that every student must attend school over the summer and spend the entire time on one subject. What subject would you choose? Explain.

✏ Which do you think is more satisfying: a cold drink on a hot summer day or a hot drink on a cold winter day? Explain.

July 12

✏ Imagine that you are walking down the street and a dalmatian stops you and asks you for directions to the nearest firehouse. Write about what happens next.

✏ It is National July Belongs to Blueberries Month. Pretend that in order to celebrate, your parent is using blueberries in all of his or her cooking. Write about the most unusual way you have eaten blueberries this month.

July 13

✏️ July is Cell Phone Courtesy Month. Write a guide for cell phone etiquette that tells how and where people should and shouldn't use their cell phones.

✏️ Imagine that you find a large diamond while playing in the sand on the beach. When you take it to a jeweler, he gives you some surprising information. Write about what happens next.

July 14

✏️ Write a silly paragraph explaining how the elephant came to have a trunk.

✏️ Describe your most memorable summer day ever.

July 15

✏️ Write a letter to your parent convincing him or her to take you on a vacation to a destination of your choice.

✏️ If you could be an ocean animal, which would you choose? Explain.

July 16

✏️ Pretend that your neighbor is going out of town and has asked you to either take care of her cat or water her garden while she is away. Which would you choose? Explain.

✏️ Imagine that as you are walking beside a pond one summer evening, you overhear a frog and a dragonfly talking. Write about the conversation they have.

July 17

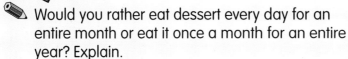

✏️ Would you rather eat dessert every day for an entire month or eat it once a month for an entire year? Explain.

✏️ Imagine that a week before school starts, you get an anonymous letter explaining that everyone will be wearing their bathing suits on the first day of school. Write about what happens next.

July 18

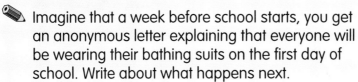

✏️ The third Sunday in July is National Ice Cream Day. Describe your favorite ice-cream treat.

✏️ Imagine that as you open your freezer door, a penguin appears and shouts for you to close the door and stop letting the heat in. Write about what happens next.

July 19

✏️ July is National Hot Dog Month. Would you rather eat a hot dog or pizza? Explain.

✏️ Write a letter to a former classmate whom you haven't seen in a long time. Be sure to tell him or her what you have been doing since you saw each other last.

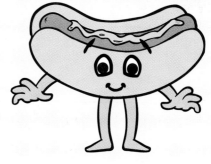

July 20

✏️ Neil Armstrong became the first man to walk on the moon on July 20, 1969. Would you like to walk on the moon? Explain.

✏️ Imagine that you sit down at a sporting event and realize that a famous person is in the seat next to you. Write about what happens next.

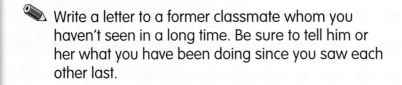

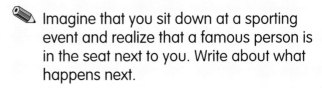

July 21

 Imagine that you just heard that your school will be closed for repairs during the upcoming school year and you will need to attend a different school. What ten questions do you have?

 Pretend that you have big plans for the summer, but your piggy bank is nearly empty. Describe how you could make money this summer.

July 22

 If you could spend the entire summer as an insect, which kind would you choose? Explain.

 Compare yourself to one of your friends. How are you alike? How are you different? Explain.

J
U
L
Y

July 23

 Imagine that you notice something strange at your town pool this summer. Suddenly every child who gets out of the pool is getting older, and every adult who gets out is getting younger. Write about what happens next.

 Are you more like a dog or a cat? Explain.

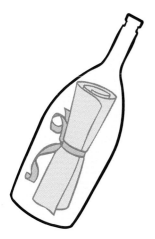

July 24

 Imagine that you found a message in a bottle on the beach. Write a return message to the original sender.

 Describe how you think you will look 20 years from today.

July 25

Happy Parents' Day!

✏️ The fourth Sunday in July is Parents' Day. Describe what you think would be the perfect way for your parent to celebrate the day.

✏️ Imagine that you just won a writing contest with a story about the worst vacation ever. Write about what happened on this vacation.

July 26

✏️ Imagine that you just opened a fortune cookie and your fortune reads "You will receive exciting news." What exciting news would you love to hear? Explain.

✏️ What five questions would you ask your favorite actor or actress if you were to meet him or her?

July 27

✏️ You've been asked to select a mascot and school colors for your school this year. Describe what you decide on and why.

✏️ Describe what is meant by the saying "once in a blue moon." Where do you think this saying came from?

July 28

✏️ Beatrix Potter, author and illustrator of *The Tale of Peter Rabbit,* was born on July 28. Write a paragraph summarizing a story called "Patricia Rabbit."

✏️ Imagine that your parents will take you on a vacation only if it is related to something you learned at school last year. Where would you go? How is it related to what you learned?

July 29

✏️ Pretend that each time your cousin comes to visit, your parent prepares his favorite meal. Unfortunately, it happens to be your least favorite. Explain what you would do.

✏️ Would you rather do something on the spur of the moment or have it planned in advance? Explain.

July 30

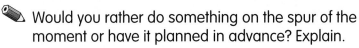

✏️ Today is the birthdate of automobile manufacturer Henry Ford. Describe the car that you would like to have when you are old enough to drive.

✏️ Write a silly paragraph explaining why most cookies are round.

July 31

✏️ Are you more like a television or a computer? Explain.

✏️ Make a list of ten or more things that are red. Imagine that you could change the color of one of these things. Which would you choose? What color would you make it? Explain.

_____
(student's name)

Journal

August

(student's name)

Journal

September

(student's name)

Journal

October

Journal

November

Journal

December

_____

(student's name)

Journal

January

Journal

February

Journal

March

(student's name)

Journal

April

_____
(student's name)

Journal

Journal

June

Journal

July

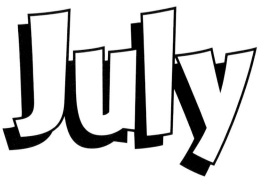

Date: _____

_____

_____

_____

_____

_____

_____

_____

_____

_____

_____

_____

_____

_____

_____

_____

_____

_____

_____

_____

_____

_____